GOD'S DIVINE PURPOSE SYSTEM

How God manifests divine purpose in your life

Jamal E. Quinn

I0170810

A publication of ML Excellence

Table of Contents

DEDICATION

This book is dedicated with love to my LORD and Savior Jesus Christ who has given me great grace, wisdom, knowledge and understanding to write about the divine purpose of God in our lives!

This book is also dedicated to all the believers in the Body of Christ that are seeking God's divine purpose for their life, and those that are fulfilling the divine purpose of God in their lives!

Last but not least it is dedicated to my wife Sheryl, my family, my close friends, and all the faithful Firm Foundation members who labor and serve faithfully with me in the work of the ministry! God has purposely put us together for such a time as this to fulfill his Kingdom plan and agenda until he returns! May God bless you richly!

INTRODUCTION

In the midst of all the chaos in the earth, God is raising up men and women of God to fulfill his divine purpose in the earth before he returns. The question is, "Are you fulfilling the divine purpose that God has ordained for your life?" Since I have been in ministry, just about every person I have met desires to know their purpose or to fulfill purpose! When we look at creation and all that is in the earth and the heavens, we see the hand of God. (Psalm 97:6) The Bible says in the beginning God created the heavens and the earth. (Gen 1:1) God in his great wisdom has created everything in the earth with a purpose and a system to maintain and sustain it. For example, God created your body with a digestive, muscular, nervous, reproductive and skeletal system.

All of these things were created with a purpose to sustain your life by our heavenly Father. Likewise as it relates to God's divine purpose for our lives, God has a purpose system that he utilizes and manifests in our lives when he calls you for service in the Kingdom of God. I refer to it as God's Divine Purpose System.

When I think about God's Divine purpose system, I am reminded of the Global Positioning System known as GPS. What is GPS? It is a satellite-based radio navigation system that uses GPS receivers to calculate the exact position, speed, distance and time for navigation devices on mobile phones, in vehicles, ships, airplanes, and government weapon systems to accurately pinpoint locations, destinations, directions and the places we need to go.

Likewise God uses his divine purpose system to get us to the destination that he has predestined, purposed, planned, promised and prophesied for our lives, using divine heavenly coordinates which are precise, detailed and exact. God is the transmitter of purpose, and we are the receiver of purpose in the earth to do his will.

Isn't that profound? The Apostle John said in John 10:27, "My sheep hear my voice, and I know them, and they follow me." Are you hearing the unmistakable voice of God as it relates to your life and purpose?

GPS also uses time, distance and speed with perfect timing to get us to our destinations, and so does God! God utilizes perfect timing to get us where we need to be in him! Each and every one of us has been created with a purpose. We are not just human beings that evolved out of amoeba over billions of years. We serve a God who has established the earth with a divine purpose and plan in mind. It is truly amazing when we think about everything that God created. God has set up the universe and created organized systems in the earth to sustain it. So as it is in the natural, so it is in the spiritual. The Apostle confirms this by saying, "However, the spiritual is not first, but the natural, and afterward the spiritual."
(1 Corinthians 15:46) NKJV. If God has created everything with a divine order and purpose, then everything that he purposed for you and me is divinely orchestrated as it relates to our lives.

When I think about my life and all that I have been through, whether it be trials, tribulations, tests, troubles, temptations and tragedies, God knew all about it. It may have been a surprise to me, but not to the Most High God. God in his great wisdom has a divine purpose and plan for each and every one of us. As we read this book, we will understand what God's Divine Purpose System is, and how he utilizes it to accomplish his will in the earth through you and me.

In this book, I make the distinction between fulfilling purpose and divine purpose. I also share from my life experiences, twenty-one years of military service in radio communications, nine years in information systems, and many years of ministry, how God orders your steps, and uses everything that you have been through, to manifest his divine purpose in your life.

CHAPTER 1

What is God's Divine Purpose System?

Have you ever used a navigation device on your phone or in your car to get to an address, a place or location where you didn't know where to go? This is what GPS or the Global Positioning System does. It is a satellite system which provides accurate location data in navigation devices to calculate the exact position, speed, time, and direction for drivers, vehicles, ships, airlines, shipping companies and trucking firms, to accurately pinpoint locations with the best route, to get from one place to another in the shortest possible time.

Many of us have used GPS on our phones and cars for navigation! In the natural we have GPS or the Global Positioning System, which is designed to get you to your destination with turn by turn directions in the shortest time possible. In the spiritual, we have God's Divine Purpose System where the LORD provides turn by turn directions to get you to your purpose and destiny in Christ according to his will.

Think about it for a moment. Everything you have been through whether good or bad, has been part of God's divine turn by turn directions to get you where you are today! When we utilize navigational systems which are run by the Global Positioning System, it tells us how far to go, when to make a turn, when we make a wrong turn, and when to turn around. It is precise and gets you where you need to go! The Word of God and the Holy Spirit provide daily, weekly, monthly and yearly turn by turn instructions in our lives. (Psalm 119:133 and John 16:13) The problem is that many of us do not listen to God's heavenly navigational voice, and some of us just plain ignore it.

We don't want to turn right even when the voice says turn right. We don't want to go left although the voice says turn left, so we end up lost because we didn't follow God's divine instructions as he navigates us to purpose and destiny in him! David the Psalmist said something so profound about the Word of God which gives us divine direction. Let's read!

"Your word is a lamp to my feet and a light to my path." Psalms 119:105 NKJV

"Order my steps in thy word: and let not any iniquity have dominion over me." Psalms 119:133 KJV

Many of us are where we are today, because we did or didn't listen to the Word of God to receive instructions or directions! There are many people today that truly desire to do the will of God, and to fulfill God's purpose for their lives. The amazing thing is that God desires that you fulfill your purpose in him! Why? Because he created you with gifts, talents and abilities for your good and for his glory! Now when we talk about God's Divine Purpose System, there are five Kingdom principles that we will define as it relates to God's divine purpose in our lives, and they are:

1. Predestination
2. Purpose
3. Plans
4. Promises
5. Prophesy

Think with me for a moment, all throughout the Bible we find the LORD using these five principles to accomplish his divine Kingdom purposes in the earth in the lives of his people.

For example, how many of us know that there are things that God has ordained and **predestined** in the earth and for our lives? (Eph 1:11) The Word of God says that all things work together for good for those that love the LORD, who are called according to his **purpose.** (Rom 8:28) The Bible also says, there are many **plans** in a man's heart, but it is the LORD's purpose that will prevail. (Prov 19:21) The Word of God also says that the **promises** of God are yes and amen, (2 Cor 1:21) because God is not a man that he should lie. (Num 23:19) We also know that what God has said in his word through **prophesy**, will come to pass according to the will, and as it relates to our lives. (Isa 55:11)

So we see that these principles are Biblical and scriptural. They pertain to everything that God has ordained to fulfill his Kingdom agenda in the earth.

We will speak in-depth on these principles later, but we must understand that one cannot truly fulfill purpose unless they are proven, or tested through a process of preparation.

How Does God Prepare Us for Purpose?

The Holy Spirit showed me that there are seven principles that will position us to fulfill God's divine purpose. I remember many years ago, one of my Pastors' said, "Some things are taught, and some things are caught." This means that there are some things that God will teach us through human vessels, and some things we must learn, and catch by the Holy Spirit! In other words, there are some things that God will do to prepare us, and there are some things we must do to position ourselves to fulfill God's divine purpose, and they are:

1. Preparation
2. Prayer
3. Passion
4. Priorities
5. Pursuit
6. Pain
7. Persecution

Preparation

Anyone who has accomplished anything significant or great in life went through a time of preparation in their lives. I have not met anyone on this earth who came forth out of the womb and immediately did great things except Jesus Christ. Have you? Even from a child we have been prepared, raised, and taught at home, and in elementary, middle, high school and eventually college. When we get a new job, there is a time of training and preparation to perform the task for which we have been hired!

Those that desire to be doctors must go to school for eight to ten years. Lawyers go to school for seven to eight years. In the military after basic training, we go to school to learn the trade for which we enlisted. In this life we are constantly learning and being educated and prepared for the future.

Even the LORD Jesus Christ went through a preparation stage before launching out into his ministry. Consider this; we read about Jesus birth and his presentation at the temple in Luke chapter 2. Then at the age of twelve he is at the temple conversing with teachers of the law. We then pick up on his life in Luke chapter 4 being tempted in the wilderness, before launching out into his ministry. Let's read these accounts of his life:

"So it was, while they were there, the days were completed for her to be delivered. And she brought forth her firstborn Son, and wrapped Him in swaddling cloths, and laid Him in a manger, because there was no room for them in the inn."
Luke 2:6-7 NKJV

"Now when the days of her purification according to the Law of Moses were completed, they brought Him to Jerusalem to present Him to the Lord."
Luke 2:22 NKJV

"And when He was twelve years old, they went up to Jerusalem according to the custom of the feast."
Luke 2:42 NKJV

"Now so it was that after three days they found Him in the temple, sitting in the midst of the teachers, both listening to them and asking them questions."
Luke 2:46 NKJV

"Then Jesus, being filled with the Holy Spirit, returned from the Jordan and was led by the Spirit into the wilderness." Luke 4:1 NKJV

After a time of preparation, and time in the desert or wilderness enduring the temptations of the devil, he launched into his earthly ministry.

When we read the Gospels we don't have a record of Jesus from age thirteen until the age of twenty nine years old. Why is the Bible silent concerning this?

Well, could it be possible that during this time Jesus was living his life and being prepared for ministry.

He was the Son of God, but he was also the Son of Man in the earth realm who did no sin, and knew no sin. The Bible says that when Jesus launched into his ministry, the people could not believe it, because he was a carpenter's son. In other words he appeared to be a normal man just like all the other men, but little did they know, God was preparing him to bring salvation to the world! Let's read!

Matthew 13:54-56 NKJV
54 When He had come to His own country, He taught them in their synagogue, so that they were astonished and said, "Where did this Man get this wisdom and these mighty works?
55 Is this not the carpenter's son? Is not His mother called Mary, and His brothers James, Joses, Simon, and Judas?
56 And His sisters, are they not all with us? Where then did this Man get all these things?"

Many of us can relate to this. You may have grown up in a town or city where everyone knew you. They probably didn't think you would accomplish anything. But later in life, God did great things in you and through you, and everyone saw the great things you did or accomplished! Only God can do this!

In the Bible we find many people who didn't appear to be great but God used them for his glory. Many of us are familiar with the story of Joseph who was the youngest of twelve sons born to Jacob. His brothers hated him because he had dreams of greatness, and because he was the favorite of his father, they plotted to kill him, not knowing that God had a great plan for his life.

"Now Israel loved Joseph more than all his children, because he was the son of his old age. Also he made him a tunic of many colors. But when his brothers saw that their father loved him more than all his brothers, they hated him and could not speak peaceably to him."
Genesis 37:3-4 NKJV

"Now when they saw him afar off, even before he came near them, they conspired against him to kill him. Then they said to one another, "Look, this dreamer is coming! Come therefore, let us now kill him and cast him into some pit; and we shall say, 'Some wild beast has devoured him.' We shall see what will become of his dreams!" Genesis 37:18-20 NKJV

The Bible says they threw him in a pit, and sold him to slave traders for twenty shekels of silver. (Gen 37:24-28)

He was then taken to Egypt, sold again to Potiphar as a slave. (Gen 37:36 and Gen 39:1) When he was in the house of Potiphar as a slave, he was faithful and successful as slave.

Genesis 39:2-4 NKJV
2 The LORD was with Joseph, and he was a successful man; and he was in the house of his master the Egyptian.
3 And his master saw that the LORD was with him and that the LORD made all he did to prosper in his hand.
4 So Joseph found favor in his sight, and served him. Then he made him overseer of his house, and all that he had he put under his authority.

But then one day, Potiphar's wife tried to seduce him and he resisted the temptation. She then lied on him, and he was thrown into prison.

"So it was, when his master heard the words which his wife spoke to him, saying, "Your servant did to me after this manner," that his anger was aroused. Then Joseph's master took him and put him into the prison, a place where the king's prisoners were confined. And he was there in the prison."
Genesis 39:19-20 NKJV

During this time, God was preparing Joseph for something great. Although his brothers hated him, he was sold into slavery, sold into Egypt, accused of rape, lied on and thrown into prison. Yet, God was preparing him to save the nation of Israel.

Joseph was eventually released from prison after interpreting Pharaoh's dream, and God used him to save the Egyptian nation from poverty and famine.

Genesis 41:37-42 NKJV
37 So the advice was good in the eyes of Pharaoh and in the eyes of all his servants.
38 And Pharaoh said to his servants, "Can we find such a one as this, a man in whom is the Spirit of God?"
39 Then Pharaoh said to Joseph, "Inasmuch as God has shown you all this, there is no one as discerning and wise as you.
40 You shall be over my house, and all my people shall be ruled according to your word; only in regard to the throne will I be greater than you."
41 And Pharaoh said to Joseph, "See, I have set you over all the land of Egypt."

42 Then Pharaoh took his signet ring off his hand and put it on Joseph's hand; and he clothed him in garments of fine linen and put a gold chain around his neck.

During the time of famine his brothers came to Egypt and eventually they were reunited and the nation of Israel was preserved. Can you see the divine purpose and hand of God in this? All that he went through and experienced was preparation to save a nation of people. Listen to the words of Joseph:

Genesis 45:7-8 NKJV
7 And God sent me before you to preserve a posterity for you in the earth, and to save your lives by a great deliverance.
8 So now it was not you who sent me here, but God; and He has made me a father to Pharaoh, and lord of all his house, and a ruler throughout all the land of Egypt.

Genesis 50:20 NKJV
20 But as for you, you meant evil against me; but God meant it for good, in order to bring it about as it is this day, to save many people alive.

Child of God, can you see that everything you have been through, and may be going through is all because of the divine purpose of God. Sometimes we think that when we are going through a challenging or tribulous time it is because of evil. Yet, God can and will it turn around for our good and his glory. God was preparing Joseph for purpose, and God will do the same for you.

Joseph is not the only one. We see preparation in the

life of King David, Israel's greatest King! We see preparation in the life of Moses, one of Israel's most revered Men of God. So we see that each and every one of us has to go through a preparation stage in life.

Preparation is important because there are things you must experience, learn and overcome as God prepares you to fulfill the divine purpose of God in your life. If you were to speak with anyone who has done anything significant in life, they would share with you their testimony of ups, downs, in's and outs, discouragements, failures and success. But in the end they did great things for God. This is why you cannot give up, quit, or throw in the towel. God may be using your experiences to prepare you to bring him glory in the earth.

Prayer

Prayer is an important principle as it relates to your life and your purpose. We find in the scriptures men and woman praying all throughout the Bible. We find many people in the Old Testament like Moses, David, and the Prophets praying. We find the disciples who became Apostles praying in the New Testament, and the greatest example of one who was always in prayer is Jesus Chris, the Son of God. Look what the scriptures say:

"Now in the morning, having risen a long while before daylight, He went out and departed to a solitary place; and there He prayed."
Mark 1:35 NKJV

"Then He spoke a parable to them that men always ought to pray and not lose heart." Luke 18:1 NKJV

"Pray without ceasing." 1 Thessalonians 5:17 NKJV

"Praying always with all prayer and supplication in the Spirit, being watchful to this end with all perseverance and supplication for all the saints."
Ephesians 6:18 NKJV

We find in the Bible that the Apostles understood the power of prayer and they had this instinct: When in trouble, pray. When intimidated, pray. When challenged, pray. When persecuted, pray. When you need help, pray. When you are sick, pray.

When you have a family issue, pray. When you need financial breakthrough, pray. When you need deliverance, pray, and when you need divine direction as it relates to your purpose, you must pray!

The thing that separates Christian churches, people, and gatherings from the world is the aroma of prayer. Remember Jesus said, "My house shall be called a house of prayer!" (Matt 21:13) Three things we must always remember!

1. Prayer takes you deeper in the things of God.
2. Prayer invokes a response from God.
3. Prayer is the anchor that holds us in the midst of the storm.

A spiritually healthy church consists of people who understand that prayer is the way to get answers in the earth! In order for us to see the power of God poured out in the church, in our communities, in our nation and in your life, you will have to pray!

If you desire to see the glory of God and the Kingdom plan of God manifested in your life, you will have to pray always without ceasing! (Luke 18:1, and 1 Thess 5:17)

Passion

Passion is very important as it relates to your life as well. When you have purpose for your life you need to understand the importance of passion. Passion is imperative to your purpose. Passion is the fuel that provides the fire and drive for what you do. In order to accomplish anything significant as it relates to your life, vision, dreams, goals or aspirations, you will need passion! When you really have a passion for something, you take ownership of it, which enables you to have a greater commitment toward it.

Commitment connects to vision, and vision gives way to creativity and purpose! In other words you should be able to say, "I am excited and committed to something because I have a passion for it." When a man or woman is passionate about something they put their all into it. People who are passionate, priority minded and prayerful always fulfill their purpose!

When I think about passion and purpose, immediately the Lord Jesus Christ comes to mind. Christ was passionate and focused for purpose. Listen to what he said about purpose!

"Now My soul is troubled, and what shall I say? Father, save me from this hour? But for this purpose I came to this hour." John 12:27 NKJV

Jesus understood the sacrifice and pain that he would have to go through, yet he stayed focused to fulfill the Father's will. Listen to words of Jesus in John 12:27:

"Now my soul is troubled, and what shall I say? Father, save me from this hour? But for this purpose I came to his hour!"

This is powerful! In other words, Jesus understood his purpose, he had passion for it, and although it would be painful, nothing was going to stop or block him from completing his assignment!

Does this describe you? Do you have passion for your purpose? I have not seen anyone who is mediocre, stagnated, complacent or slothful do anything significant in the earth!

I have observed in life that the only way a business, group, team or church can be truly successful is to have a zeal and passion for what they do. In order for leaders in ministry to fulfill their calling and be successful in the work of the ministry, they must have a passion and focus as it relates to the mission and vision of that organization.

Even as an individual, you must be passionate about your purpose, which means you must be focused. Let's define passion and focus together.

What is passion? It is zeal, love, or an eager desire. What is focus? - It is a state or condition permitting clear perception or understanding, a point of concentration, directed attention or emphasis.

So when you put these two together there is a zeal, love or eager desire and a focus which enables you to get a clear picture toward a particular thing, or goal that you are trying to achieve.

So if you lose your passion and your focus you can get distracted, discouraged, and frustrated. Many times you will find people who have potential, but lack passion and focus.

If you are purpose and goal minded with passion, coupled with faith, humility, and a servant's heart, it would be impossible to not fulfill your purpose! Remember, as it relates to your purpose you must be passionate and focused as it relates to the Kingdom plan of God for your life! Always have a passion for what you do! Passion will ignite a fire inside you to keep you focused for purpose.

Pursuit

"As the deer pants for the water brooks, so pants my soul for You, O God. My soul thirsts for God, for the living God. When shall I come and appear before God?" Psalms 42:1-2 NKJV

When you think about the word "pursuit" what comes to mind? The dictionary defines pursuit as; the action of following or pursuing someone or something, or an effort to secure, attain, or quest. Other words are chasing, pursuing, stalking, chase after, seek or search for. In Psalm 42, the Psalmist gives us a vivid picture of a deer thirsting for water at a water brook.

He then contrasts the deer's panting and thirst for water as the Psalmist thirsts for the living God. He appears to be seeking, hungering and thirsting after God. He also says, "When shall I come and appear before God?" In this passage of scripture, there is a pursuit of God. He wants more of God. He desires more of God.

Is this how you feel about God as it relates to purpose? Are you hungering and thirsting for God? Do you desire to do the will of God? People say they want to fulfill purpose, but their actions speak otherwise! People in the world hunger and thirst for money, sex, material things, fame and fortune, but the divine purpose minded man and woman is in pursuit of God, and they hunger and thirst after his righteousness.

Jesus said the following:

"Blessed are those who hunger and thirst for righteousness, for they shall be filled."
Matthew 5:6 NKJV

Did you hear that? When you hunger and thirst after righteousness you shall be filled. When you hunger and thirst after spiritual things you will be filled. When you seek after God you will find him.

The scriptures say in Matthew 7:7-11 NKJV
7 "Ask, and it will be given to you; seek, and you will find; knock, and it will be opened to you.
8 For everyone who asks receives, and he who seeks finds, and to him who knocks it will be opened.
9 Or what man is there among you who, if his son asks for bread, will give him a stone?
10 Or if he asks for a fish, will he give him a serpent?
11 If you then, being evil, know how to give good gifts to your children, how much more will your Father who is in heaven give good things to those who ask Him!

David said something profound in Psalm 34:14:

"Depart from evil, and do good; seek peace, and pursue it." Psalms 34:14 KJV

Pursuit and seek are unique words but the definitions have the same meaning in a sense when you put them together.

The Psalmist tells us to seek after peace and pursue it. In other words look for it, search for it, chase or follow after it, and desire to obtain it.
In Matt 6:33, the LORD said:

"But seek first the kingdom of God and His righteousness, and all these things shall be added to you." Matthew 6:33 NKJV

Does this describe your desire to know God and to accomplish the purpose for your life? Are you seeking first the Kingdom of God and his righteousness? Are you pursuing the things of God for your life?

The LORD told the people of God something interesting in Jeremiah 29:

Jeremiah 29:11-14 KJV
11 For I know the thoughts that I think toward you, says the LORD, thoughts of peace, and not of evil, to give you an expected end.
12 Then shall you call upon me, and you shall go and pray unto me, and I will hearken unto you.
13 And you shall seek me, and find me, when you shall search for me with all your heart.
14 And I will be found of you, says the LORD: and I will turn away your captivity, and I will gather you from all the nations, and from all the places where I have driven you, says the LORD; and I will bring you again into the place where I caused you to be carried away captive.

When we really look at this scripture, the LORD is telling the people of God that despite what you are going through right now. My thoughts toward you are of peace and not of evil, to give you a hope and a future. In other words, I have a purpose for you and the end of the matter is going to work in your favor.

The LORD also reminded the people of God through the Prophet Jeremiah that the purpose, plans and promises that he established for them would come to pass, but they had to do four things:

1. Call unto me.
2. Pray to me.
3. Seek me.
4. Search for me with all of your heart.

This is what pursuing God is all about; calling on the name of the LORD, praying, seeking, and searching for him with all of your heart! Does this describe you? When this scripture was written to the tribe of Judah, they were about to go into captivity, but God said I have a purpose for you and it will come to pass, but you must expectation in your heart! As a matter of fact, verse 13 says, "And you shall seek me, and find me, when you shall search for me with all your heart."

Jesus told the disciples in Matt 7:7-8, "Ask and you shall receive, seek and you shall find, knock and the door shall be opened."
This is what pursuit is all about! I want to encourage you to keep seeking, searching and pursuing God. When you do, you will not only find what you are pursuing, but you will be found by the LORD!

Priorities

When we look at scripture, we find that men and women, who were called by God understood the importance of the call of God on their life. The question I want to ask you is, "Do you understand the importance of priorities in your life as it relates to the Gospel of the Kingdom?"

The LORD Jesus once told the disciples in Matt 10:37-39:

Matthew 10:37-39 NKJV
37 He who loves father or mother more than me is not worthy of Me. And he who loves son or daughter more than me is not worthy of Me.
38 And he who does not take his cross and follow after me is not worthy of Me.
39 He who finds his life will lose it, and he who loses his life for my sake will find it.

Now understand that this is not a popular scripture because all of us would agree that family is important. When this passage of scripture is taught or preached, many people will take it out of context. What the LORD was saying in this passage speaks about priorities in our life as it relates following Christ. Jesus said if you love anyone or anything more than me, you are not worthy of me.

Why would Jesus say this? Because in order to fulfill the Kingdom purpose of God for your life, it will take sacrifice and priorities. The LORD understands the importance of family and would never do anything to hinder that, but understand that his Kingdom agenda and purpose in the earth must go forth. This is why the scripture says, "Many are called but few are chosen." (Matt 22:14)

I can recall when I was in the military. Sometimes my Navy responsibilities and assignment called for me to deploy, and be away from my family for three to six months. One assignment required me to be overseas away from my family for one whole year. Then when it was completed, I was sent to another city for two and a half years where I had to commute to my home on the weekends.

Some of us would say, Pastor, that's just too much, but you must understand, that's what I signed up for! It wasn't that I didn't love my family, but my responsibilities as a military member dictated my priorities and assignment in the military, and my family understood this! It is the same in ministry. Your assignment dictates your responsibilities and your priorities!

There were many people who got out of the military because the assignments and responsibilities where too much. There is nothing wrong with that! It's all based on what you believe is best for you and your family. It's the same in ministry as it relates to purpose in Christ. If it is too much, God understands.

All you have to do is make a decision! This is easier said than done, but God desires the best for your life, and he has given us freewill to make decisions for our lives!

When the disciples were called to follow Jesus, look at what their response was in Matthew 4:18-22:

18 And Jesus, walking by the Sea of Galilee, saw two brothers, Simon called Peter, and Andrew his brother, casting a net into the sea; for they were fishermen.
19 Then He said to them, "Follow Me, and I will make you fishers of men."
20 They immediately left their nets and followed Him.
21 Going on from there, He saw two other brothers, James the son of Zebedee, and John his brother, in the boat with Zebedee their father, mending their nets. He called them,
22 and immediately they left the boat and their father, and followed Him.

The disciples understood that although they were fishermen who were businessmen, they were called to be fishers of men. What they were called to do in following the Messiah dictated their priorities as it related to the Kingdom purpose, and plan of God for their life.

We must understand that many people never fulfill purpose because they don't understand priorities in their life. I have found that people who are late, tardy and unprepared, do not understand the importance of priorities! The LORD once told a parable about a rich man, and showed us how priorities determine our decisions. Lets read!

A rich man once asked the LORD a very important question:

Luke 18:18-23 KJV
18 Now a certain ruler asked Him, saying, "Good Teacher, what shall I do to inherit eternal life?"

19 So Jesus said to him, "Why do you call me good? No one is good but One, that is, God.
20 Do you know the commandments, Do not commit adultery, Do not kill, Do not steal, Do not bear false witness, Honor your father and your mother.
21 And he said, All these have I kept from my youth up.

Jesus response was profound, listen to what he told the man:

22 Now when Jesus heard these things, he said unto him, yet you lack one thing: sell all that you have, and distribute unto the poor, and you shall have treasure in heaven: and come, follow me.
23 And when he heard this, he was very sorrowful: for he was very rich.

When you look at this story, the young man had potential to do great things, and could have been a disciple of the LORD Jesus Christ, but he had his priorities wrong. He loved the riches of his life more than the purpose and plan of God for his life.

Jesus said something so profound in Matt 6:33 "Seek first the Kingdom of God and his righteousness, and all these things shall be added unto you."

The Lord has given us the key to success in whatever we aspire or desire to do. It is putting him first, seeking him first, or putting God first! Let me ask you something? Is God first or education first? Is God first or your bills first? Is God first or your business first? Remember your priorities reveal really what is first in your life, and many times we wonder why we are so tired, stressed out, and burned out.

One of the reasons is because we have not learned the scriptural principle of firstfruits in our lives which will bless you beyond measure! If you put God first, he will put you first! Let's take a look at some scripture!

Proverbs 3:9-10 NKJV
9 Honor the LORD with your possessions, and with the firstfruits of all your increase;
10 So your barns will be filled with plenty, and your vats will overflow with new wine.

We see from the scripture that when we prioritize and put God first, he always remembers us!

Jesus even knew from a child that he had a special purpose in the earth. Many of us know the story of Jesus leaving his parents and going back to the temple to listen to teachers and asking them questions.

Luke 2:46-49 NKJV
46 Now so it was that after three days they found Him in the temple, sitting in the midst of the teachers, both listening to them and asking them questions.
47 And all who heard Him were astonished at His understanding and answers.
48 So when they saw Him, they were amazed; and His mother said to Him, "Son, why have you done this to us? Look, your father and I have sought you anxiously."
49 And He said to them, "Why did you seek me? Did you not know that I must be about My Father's business?"

Prioritization as it relates to purpose means that you are serious about your purpose in Christ. There is absolutely no way you can fulfill purpose in Christ, if your priorities do not line up with the will of God. Purpose driven people understand prioritization. They understand that the will of God is more important than their will.

Remember what I said about the Global Positioning system, it encompasses time, distance and speed to get you to your destination in the most accurate and fastest time possible When your priorities don't line up with the perfect will of God, you will find yourself moving slowly toward your purpose, and you wonder why things have not shifted in your life. If you shift your priorities you shift your life, if you shift your life you shift your purpose.

Some of us have two speeds when it comes to the things of God! Slow and slower! I don't know about you, but I don't know when God is going to call me home, so I got a short window to fulfill purpose! Jesus had three years to fulfill divine purpose and then the Father said come on back home Son.

A mediocre, procrastinating, lackluster, lackadaisical attitude with no passion or prioritization will never produce purpose, or miracles in the Kingdom of God.

The fact of the matter is that we don't know when our time is up, so we don't have time to move like Cecil turtle! This is the season to press in, to be diligent, to be urgent, and to be about the Fathers business. We must understand that this gospel bus is moving, and people get on, people get off, people miss the bus, people get on the wrong bus, and they transfer to other buses, but this bus must keep on moving. I heard people tell me years ago, Pastor I love you, I love this church, I got your back, and I will never leave you. Well, I don't see them, and haven't heard from them, but I got to keep on driving till I see Jesus! Praise God!

The Bible says in Matthew 11:12 and from the days of John the Baptist until now the kingdom of heaven suffers violence, and the violent take it by force."

I'm not talking about guns, but we need to get violent with prayer, some of us need to get violent in the word of God, some of us need to get violent in our time, some of us need to get violent in witnessing, and some of us are just too passive as it pertains to life in Christ.

When boss man on the job says go, or do this, we move quickly. When God says do something, you hesitate, you need two or three witnesses, and a sign from heaven like Gideon, but God wants you to seek first his Kingdom and his righteousness so that he can release the blessings and God ideas to you.

Truth be told, you know why that God idea or Kingdom innovation hasn't come to pass, because of your priorities. If God can't trust you with $100.00 or $1000.00, why would he put $1 million in your hand? Most people will quit their job, buy their favorite car, buy a new house, pay off some bills, go on a cruise, come back to church after two weeks on vacation and put 10 dollars in the offering plate. Wow, talk about wrong priorities! Now, that's not all people, but some people don't understand the importance of priorities, especially when it all belongs to God anyway! Somebody say priorities! Believe me people of God, priorities are important as it relates to your purpose! Don't miss God because your priorities are more important than the Kingdom of God!

And listen, I understand the busyness of life! I have been away from my family for six months on a Navy ship, one year in the Middle East, two and a half years away from my family on military duty, but I knew that I had purpose, and God was preparing me for something great! Before I got out in 2005, they wanted me to stay, and I could have been promoted with more rank, but my priorities were my family and the Gospel of the Kingdom.

Listen people of God, today, repent of your lack of priorities as it relates to your relationship in Christ! Not church, but in him, because when you prioritize in him, everything else falls into place! And guess what? There is nothing you have done, no seed that you have sown, no labor that you have performed that will not reap a harvest in your life when you do it as unto the Lord!~

If you do it for man, you get a reward. You get a pat on the back, or a word of thanks, but if you put God first and do it for Jesus Christ, expect all these things that you desire and aspire to be added unto you and your family in Jesus Name!

I want you to know that everyone under the sound of my voice has been brought into the Kingdom for such a time as this. Remember that God is not in your comfort zone. God is about his Kingdom business agenda which is Kingdom expansion in which we are all a part of!

I want you to know today, you don't have time to waste. Each day your life gets shorter! And your window to fulfill purpose gets shorter! It's time to seek first the Kingdom of heaven, and his righteousness so that all these things that God has prepared for you, before the foundations of the earth can come to pass in Jesus name!

Pain

If there is one thing that many people have experienced in their lives as it relates to preparation, purpose, and the plan of God for their life is pain. If you live long enough, at some point in your life you will experience some pain. Anyone who has been called of God will tell you that at some point in their life they experienced pain or suffering.

There are many people in the Bible who fulfilled the call and purpose of God, and experienced some kind of pain in their lives. When we look at the lives of many of God's people in the Bible we see much pain and suffering, but we also see the purpose of God manifested out of it. For example, the people of God in Egypt, the people of God in captivity for seventy years, Moses, David, Daniel, Job, Jabez, Paul, The Apostles and even Jesus Christ!

I often think about those that who came before us who experienced pain! Many people died for civil rights and freedom, and many people fought and died in many wars on behalf of our country.

What about King David a shepherd boy who was anointed to be the next King of Israel? They celebrated him at one point, then after he was anointed King, a turn of events happened in his life. Saul who was the King at that time tried to kill him. David then fled for his life and was on the run hiding in the mountains and in caves surrounding the Dead Sea.

It is then that David began asking the tough questions of life. If I am King, why am I running for my life living in caves? David was frustrated, and he wrote about it in the Psalms. Although Saul stopped at nothing to kill David, David had the opportunity to kill Saul who had stopped in a cave to relieve himself. David crept up behind him unawares and cut a small portion of his robe, to show him he could have harmed him, but never followed through on it.

1 Samuel 24:5-6 NKJV
5 Now it happened afterward that David's heart troubled him because he had cut Saul's robe.
6 And he said to his men, "The LORD forbid that I should do this thing to my master, the LORD's anointed, to stretch out my hand against him, seeing he is the anointed of the LORD."

This is a lesson that many of God's people should learn. Even in the midst of pain and tough times, don't take matters into your own hands. God is in control! David's time alone with God forged his exemplary character and unflinching faith. Through loneliness and struggle, David learned to be fully dependent on God. You will find in many of the Psalms that David is pouring his heart out to the Lord because of his pain, hurt, disappointment, and discouragement over the circumstances in his life.

Has anyone ever experienced pain from a relationship, from false accusation, or even an accident? Many times when we are going through, it appears that God doesn't hear our prayers, and sometimes we feel as if there is no comfort for the pain that we experience in our lives.

But Paul said something profound in 2 Cor 4:17-18:

17 For our light affliction, which is but for a moment, is working for us a far more exceeding and eternal weight of glory,
18 while we do not look at the things which are seen, but at the things which are not seen. For the things which are seen are temporary, but the things which are not seen are eternal.

Even though we don't know why we go through what we go through, we must understand that we have divine purpose for our lives, and that our light affliction is but for a moment, and is working for us a far more exceeding and eternal weight of glory! In other words, God is working it out for our good and his glory! The Psalmist said that weeping may endure for a night but joy comes in the morning! (Psalm 30:5)

Many of us know the story of Joseph who went through much pain but God used it for his glory! Joseph was the favorite of his father's eleven other sons, and was hated by his brothers. They called him a dreamer, spoke bad about him, plotted to kill him, stripped him of his nice jacket, threw him in a pit, and then sold him to slaver traders for 20 pieces of silver. He was then taken into Egypt and sold into slavery again. Now when he got into Egypt, despite all he went through, He was diligent and God gave him favor!   He was then accused him of rape, and he was thrown into prison for three years. Many of you would agree that Joseph had some pain! (Gen 39:1-23)

But Joseph knew there was purpose for his life. Because he had a dream that he was going to do great things, just like many of you reading this book!

Although you have been through much pain, you know deep down that God has ordained for you to do something special in the earth that will bless the lives of countless people. This is why you must go through, to get to what God has purposed in your life!

One thing we can all agree on is that pain is not fun, pain is not comfortable, and pain is not a process that anyone is willing to go through. Pain will humble you, pain will cause you to pray, and pain will cause you to seek God if you really want to be healed! But as we discussed, God will allow some things to happen in our lives so that he can perfect us for his perfect will and purpose.

You will find throughout scripture that God has used the process of pain in an individual's life to mold them, and shape them into the perfected vessel they are today, and to save countless lives.

Many of you can testify that pain has got you to the place where you are today. Many people can give you testimony after testimony of how painful circumstances in their lives have taught them life lessons and spiritual truths that have enabled them to be a better person, and to fulfill the purpose of God upon their life.

When we think about Joseph's life, and all the pain that he went through was for a reason. Listen to what he told his brothers:

Genesis 45:4-8 NKJV
4 And Joseph said to his brothers, "Please come near to me." So they came near. Then he said: "I am Joseph your brother, whom you sold into Egypt.

5 But now, do not therefore be grieved or angry with yourselves because you sold me here; for God sent me before you to preserve life.

6 For these two years the famine has been in the land, and there are still five years in which there will be neither plowing nor harvesting.

7 And God sent me before you to preserve a posterity for you in the earth, and to save your lives by a great deliverance.

8 So now it was not you who sent me here, but God; and He has made me a father to Pharaoh, and lord of all his house, and a ruler throughout all the land of Egypt.

Did you read that? Joseph said, "God sent me before you to preserve posterity for you in the earth, and to save your lives by a great deliverance!" Not only that, but Joseph said, "So it was not you, but God who sent me here!" You mean to tell me that all the pain that Joseph experienced was because God allowed it for a greater purpose? Yes, this is true. God has a greater purpose than any of us can fathom, and he allows us to go through, to accomplish his divine purpose in the earth!

Joseph went on to say:

Genesis 50:20-21 NKJV
20 But as for you, you meant evil against me; but God meant it for good, in order to bring it about as it is this day, to save many people alive.

21 Now therefore, do not be afraid; I will provide for you and your little ones." And he comforted them and spoke kindly to them.

So Joseph went through all of that pain to bless someone else's life and to save their lives. God is the one that allowed him to go through all of that pain, and he is not alone. God has allowed you and me to go through much in our lives for the greater good!

Listen to the Apostle Paul:

2 Corinthians 1:3-6 NKJV
3 Blessed be the God and Father of our Lord Jesus Christ, the Father of mercies and God of all comfort,
4 who comforts us in all our tribulation, that we may be able to comfort those who are in any trouble, with the comfort with which we ourselves are comforted by God.
5 For as the sufferings of Christ abound in us, so our consolation also abounds through Christ.
6 Now if we are afflicted, it is for your consolation and salvation, which is effective for enduring the same sufferings which we also suffer. Or if we are comforted, it is for your consolation and salvation.

This is a Biblical concept that we don't hear much about. God will comfort us in our trouble so that we are able to comfort others! Isn't this what the cross was all about? Jesus Christ endured the most abominable pain and scorn that an innocent man could ever experience at the cross of our behalf, so that we could be free from the curse of the law of sin and death.

Listen to what Isaiah said about the LORD Jesus Christ in Isaiah 53:3-10:

3 He is despised and rejected by men, a man of sorrows and acquainted with grief. And we hid, as it

were, our faces from Him; He was despised, and we did not esteem Him.

4 Surely He has borne our griefs and carried our sorrows; yet we esteemed Him stricken, smitten by God, and afflicted.

5 But He was wounded for our transgressions, He was bruised for our iniquities; the chastisement for our peace was upon Him, and by His stripes we are healed.

6 All we like sheep have gone astray; we have turned, every one, to his own way; and the LORD has laid on Him the iniquity of us all.

7 He was oppressed and He was afflicted, Yet He opened not His mouth; He was led as a lamb to the slaughter, and as a sheep before its shearers is silent, So He opened not His mouth.

8 He was taken from prison and from judgment, and who will declare His generation? For He was cut off from the land of the living; for the transgressions of my people He was stricken.

9 And they made His grave with the wicked—but with the rich at His death, Because He had done no violence, nor was any deceit in His mouth.

10 Yet it pleased the LORD to bruise Him; He has put Him to grief. When you make His soul an offering for sin, He shall see His seed, He shall prolong His days, and the pleasure of the LORD shall prosper in His hand.

Our LORD Jesus Christ experienced pain and suffering at the hands of sinful men and was crucified. Yet it was all part of the plan and purpose of God. Let's read what the scripture says:

Matthew 16:21 NKJV
21 From that time Jesus began to show to His

disciples that He must go to Jerusalem, and suffer many things from the elders and chief priests and scribes, and be killed, and be raised the third day.

Jesus knew the purpose for which he came to the earth would result in pain and suffering for the sins of the world. He felt the pain, he knew there would be much pain, and he thought about it in the Garden of Gethsemane.

Luke 22:41-44 NKJV
41 And He was withdrawn from them about a stone's throw, and He knelt down and prayed,
42 saying, "Father, if it is your will, take this cup away from me; nevertheless not my will, but yours, be done."
43 Then an angel appeared to Him from heaven, strengthening Him.
44 And being in agony, He prayed more earnestly. Then His sweat became like great drops of blood falling down to the ground.

Even the Son of God knew the pain that would result at the cross of Calvary, and Jesus said, "Father, if it is your will, take this cup from me, nevertheless, not my will but your will be done."

The Bible says that Jesus was in so much pain and agony that an angel came and strengthened him. The Bible also says that he was in agony and prayed more earnestly, and his sweat was like drops of blood falling to the ground. (Verse 44) Child of God, we have no clue what the LORD was going through, but the Bible gives us a glimpse of the pain that Christ when through before and at the cross!

If you could talk to many people in ministry they could tell you of the pain that they have experienced and endured. All through my life from a child to an adult I have experienced some kind of pain, whether it was sickness in my body, emotional pain from my mother's death when I was eight years old, my father and grandmother's death in 2013, one month apart, and then five months later in 2014, my wife had a serious medical situation which was very painful!

The Apostle Paul gave us a glimpse of the pain he endured while preaching the Gospel. Listen to his testimony:

2 Corinthians 11:23-27 NKJV
23 Are they ministers of Christ?—I speak as a fool—I am more: in labors more abundant, in stripes above measure, in prisons more frequently, in deaths often.
24 From the Jews five times I received forty stripes minus one.
25 Three times I was beaten with rods; once I was stoned; three times I was shipwrecked; a night and a day I have been in the deep;
26 in journeys often, in perils of waters, in perils of robbers, in perils of my own countrymen, in perils of the Gentiles, in perils in the city, in perils in the wilderness, in perils in the sea, in perils among false brethren;
27 in weariness and toil, in sleeplessness often, in hunger and thirst, in fasting's often, in cold and nakedness.

Paul also talked about more pain as well as result of his ministry for Christ:

2 Corinthians 12:7-10 NKJV

7 And lest I should be exalted above measure by the abundance of the revelations, a thorn in the flesh was given to me, a messenger of Satan to buffet me, lest I be exalted above measure.

8 Concerning this thing I pleaded with the Lord three times that it might depart from me.

9 And He said to me, "My grace is sufficient for you, for my strength is made perfect in weakness." Therefore god can use
 I will rather boast in my infirmities, that the power of Christ may rest upon me.

10 Therefore I take pleasure in infirmities, in reproaches, in needs, in persecutions, in distresses, for Christ's sake. For when I am weak, then I am strong.

Although we may experience pain in our lives, God will give us the grace to get through it. When the LORD responded that his grace was sufficient, and his strength was made perfect in weakness. Paul said "Well if Gods strength is made perfect in weakness, I am going to boast in my infirmities. For when I am weak then I am strong."

Pain is a part of the process as it relates to purpose. I say this with humility because no one likes to experience pain and suffering, but no man is greater than the Master Jesus Christ, and no student is above the teacher. If Christ experienced pain, we will have to do the same. No man or woman can be anointed with the Christ anointing without experiencing pain, whether it be physically, spiritually, financially, mentally or emotionally.

I have read that olives must be pressed in order to get the precious olive oil out of them. There is revelation in this statement, because Jesus was in the Garden of Gethsemane prior to being arrested, and the Bible says he was in much sorrow and deeply distressed almost onto death! Gethsemane in the Greek means "oil press." In other words Jesus was being pressed in his spirit and was experiencing so much pain in his heart for what he was about to go through.

Matthew 26:36-38 NKJV
36 Then Jesus came with them to a place called Gethsemane, and said to the disciples, "Sit here while I go and pray over there."
37 And He took with Him Peter and the two sons of Zebedee, and He began to be sorrowful and deeply distressed.
38 Then He said to them, "My soul is exceedingly sorrowful, even to death. Stay here and watch with Me."

Can you sense the pain that Christ was feeling before going to the cross? Jesus, the Son of the Most High God was beaten and crucified for you and me. Just as an olive is pressed to release the precious oil, he was beaten and crucified, and he shed his blood on our behalf at the cross!

The Pain of Jabez

There is another story in 1 Chronicles 4: 9-10 about a man named Jabez whose mother named him sorrow, because she bore him in sorrow. Listen to his testimony in 1 Chronicles 4:9:

9 Now Jabez was more honorable than his brothers, and his mother called his name Jabez, saying, "Because I bore him in sorrow."

The King James Version translation says she bore him in sorrow. The Bible doesn't tell us what that sorrow was, but Jabez felt the pain and weight of his name.

We should be careful of the names that we call others or even name our children, because prophetically they can take on that prophecy. Look at what the Bible says about names.

"A good name is rather to be chosen than great riches, and loving favor rather than silver and gold." Proverbs 22:1 KJV

"A good name is better than precious ointment; and the day of death than the day of one's birth." Ecclesiastes 7:1 KJV

Although Jabez felt pain and sorrow in his life, one day he called on the Yahweh, the God of Abraham, Isaac and Jacob and look what happened in verse 10:

"And Jabez called on the God of Israel, saying, Oh that you would bless me indeed, and enlarge my coast, and that your hand might be with me, and that you would keep me from evil, that it may not grieve me! And God granted him that which he requested." 1 Chronicles 4:10 KJV

Although Jabez experienced some pain or sorrow in his life, he called on God and the LORD answered his prayer!

Someone once said that the key to blessing and breakthrough is persevering through pain or brokenness. If you are not willing to be broken you will never experience blessing and breakthrough. And to tell the truth many times we don't know what God is up to in our lives, and we just don't understand God's ways. We must understand that God knows what you need, to get you where he wants you to be! Despite what we may go through in life, God will heal, restore and make us whole for his Kingdom purposes in the earth.

You need to know that what you have been through is all part of the process to perfect you for purpose! And many times we see people were they are now, but you don't know what they have been through.

There is a saying, "People may see your present glory, but they don't know your story." In order for you to come into your purpose, God allows you to go through a process of pain which humbles and matures you. You cannot bypass the process of pain to be used and called of God. The scripture says that many are called but few are chosen. (Matt 22:14)

I have found that throughout scripture God has used the process of pain to perfect those he has called and used them for his glory. Remember our ways are not God's ways, and neither our thoughts his thoughts! (Isaiah 55:9) God has always used pain to rebuke, chastise, strengthen, humble, and to build up the people of God. You will find throughout scripture that God uses the process of pain in an individual's life to mold them, and shape them into perfected vessels to save countless lives. I want to encourage you that no matter what you go through in life, God is using your pain to perfect you for a greater purpose in your life.

Persecution

One of the things we find as it relates to the church is that persecution is increasing. There has always been persecution against the church, but in these last days there is a significant increase in many parts of the world where the gospel is being preached with power. Persecution has been a part of the church since it was founded. Jesus dealt with persecution. The Disciples who became Apostles dealt with persecution. The Apostle Paul was persecuted, and we even find that one of the seven churches of Revelation (The church of Smyrna) was a persecuted church. Let's read Rev 2:10.

"Do not fear any of those things which you are about to suffer. Indeed, the devil is about to throw some of you into prison, that you may be tested, and you will have tribulation ten days. Be faithful until death, and I will give you the crown of life."
Revelation 2:10 NKJV

Jesus told the church of Smyrna to not fear because of the things they would suffer. He mentions the words prison, tested, and tribulation, which tells us that they would indeed experience some persecution! He then tells the church to be faithful until death, and they will receive the crown of life.

Peter in the book of Mark told Jesus that they left everything to follow him, and the LORD Jesus told the disciples that they would be blessed as a result of their sacrifice in following him, but there would also be persecutions.

Let's read Mark 10:28-30 NKJV:

28 Then Peter began to say to Him, "See, we have left all and followed you."
29 So Jesus answered and said, "Assuredly, I say to you, there is no one who has left house or brothers or sisters or father or mother or wife or children or lands, for my sake and the gospel's,
30 who shall not receive a hundredfold now in this time, houses and brothers and sisters and mothers and children and lands, **with persecutions**—and in the age to come, eternal life.

Did you get that? You will indeed be blessed but there will also be some persecutions because of our testimony for Jesus Christ. The Apostle Paul confirms this in 2 Tim 3:12 by saying:

"Yes, and all who desire to live godly in Christ Jesus will suffer persecution." 2 Timothy 3:12 NKJV

The Apostle Paul that when you live godly for Jesus Christ you will suffer persecution. No one desires to be persecuted but we find that the LORD Jesus and the Apostle Paul spoke about this. One of the things we must understand is if they persecuted Christ, they will persecute us as well. Sometimes people don't understand this, but they that live godly in Jesus Christ will suffer persecution! Why? Because you are in his world but not of this world! Listen to what the LORD said:

John 15:19 NKJV
19 If you were of the world, the world would love its own. Yet because you are not of the world, but I chose you out of the world, therefore the world hates you.

In other words because you follow the truth of Christ, the world will hate you. The world has its own system in which it embraces those that follow the worlds system. When you were born again, you were translated into the Kingdom of God. The scripture confirms it.

John 3:5-6 KJV
5 Jesus answered, Verily, verily, I say unto thee, except a man be born of water and of the Spirit, he cannot enter into the kingdom of God.
6 That which is born of the flesh is flesh; and that which is born of the Spirit is spirit.

Colossians 1:12-14 KJV
12 Giving thanks unto the Father, which hath made us to be partakers of the inheritance of the saints in light:
13 Who hath delivered us from the power of darkness, and hath translated us into the kingdom of his dear Son:
14 In whom we have redemption through his blood, even the forgiveness of sins.

Jesus even confirms it in his signs of the times discourse:

The LORD Jesus told the disciples something so profound as he prophetically shared with them the signs of the times in Matthew chapter 24, and also mentions persecution.

"Then shall they deliver you up to be afflicted, and shall kill you: and ye shall be hated of all nations for my name's sake." Matthew 24:9 KJV

We find today that when we preach the Gospel of the Kingdom and our LORD Jesus Christ, it is an offense to many. You can say any other name or practice any other religion, but the moment you mention Jesus, or preach Jesus, persecution is sure. As it relates to purpose we must be bold, confident, strong, and know that the LORD will be with us, and will not leave us nor forsake us!

There is a book I read many years ago entitled Foxe's Book of Martyrs. This book will bring you to tears. The book written by John Fox; details the life, suffering, and triumphant deaths of the early Christians and Protestant martyrs who suffered persecution for their faith under the Catholic Church.

The writer of Hebrews mentions some the persecutions that believers endured as a result of their faith as well.

Hebrews 11:36-39 KJV
36 And others had trial of cruel mockings and scourgings, yea, moreover of bonds and imprisonment:
37 They were stoned, they were sawn asunder, were tempted, and were slain with the sword: they wandered about in sheepskins and goatskins; being destitute, afflicted, tormented;
38 (Of whom the world was not worthy :) they wandered in deserts, and in mountains, and in dens and caves of the earth.
39 And these all, having obtained a good report through faith, received not the promise.

One thing we must understand is that Jesus said that we would be persecuted for our faith. As it relates to purpose in Christ, we will experience some persecution in the world because of the ungodliness of men. So we find that when we are walking in divine purpose we will indeed experience some sort of persecution.

There are believers today who are experiencing persecution in the Middle East, India, China, and many other countries in the world. As we speak, persecution is taking place right now. We will also see an increase of persecution in the United States for our faith as the coming of Christ draws near. Nevertheless, we must keep the faith and fulfill our purpose in this generation in preaching the gospel to all nations in Jesus name! Let us remember what the LORD Jesus said to the church of Smyrna. This should encourage us all.

"Do not fear any of those things which you are about to suffer. Indeed, the devil is about to throw some of you into prison, that you may be tested, and you will have tribulation ten days. **Be faithful until death, and I will give you the crown of life.**" **Revelation 2:10 NKJV**

CHAPTER 2

PREDESTINED

"Moreover whom He predestined, these He also
called; whom He called, these He also justified; and
whom He justified, these He also glorified."
Romans 8:30 NKJV

As we discuss God's Divine Purpose System, we
have looked at seven principles that prepare and
position us for purpose in Christ. Now we will move
on and discuss in these next five chapters, principles
that relate to God's divine purpose in our lives. These
are the things that God has predestined, purposed,
planned, promised and prophesied in his Word
concerning our lives in Christ Jesus our LORD.

Let's talk about predestination for a moment! Earlier
in this book we discussed the differences between
predestination and free will. Predestination is also
known as election which teaches that God has
already set everything up in the earth and we are just
walking it out. Free will says that everything we do is
based on our decisions and choices we make in life.

The truth of the matter is that both of them are true.
Because God has given us the freedom to choose, and
God has made us free moral agents in whom we can
decide to make decisions to follow him, or not to
follow him. I know this to be true, because although
God saved you, he will not make you pray, he will not

make you read your bible. He will not make you do anything, but has given us choice! Although he knows full well what you are going to do!

Having said that, there are some things that God has ordained that will come to pass, and must take place according to the counsel of his own will, and there is nothing that you and me can do about it.

A good scriptural example is in Romans where the Apostle Paul is speaking about what God has ordained as it relates to Abraham's seed; Isaac and Jacob.

Romans 9:9-18 KJV
9 For this is the word of promise, at this time will I come, and Sarah shall have a son.
10 And not only this; but when Rebecca also had conceived by one, even by our father Isaac;
11 (For the children being not yet born, neither having done any good or evil, **that the purpose of God according to election might stand, not of works, but of him that calls;)**
12 It was said unto her, the elder shall serve the younger.
13 As it is written, Jacob have I loved, but Esau have I hated.
14 What shall we say then? Is there unrighteousness with God? God forbid.
15 For he said to Moses, I will have mercy on whom I will have mercy, and I will have compassion on whom I will have compassion.

16 So then it is not of him that wills, nor of him that runs, but of God that shows mercy.

17 For the scripture says unto Pharaoh, even for this same purpose have I raised thee up, that I might shew my power in thee, and that my name might be declared throughout all the earth.

18 Therefore hath he mercy on whom he will have mercy, and whom he will he hardens.

The Apostle Paul is speaking about the promise made to Abraham and Sarah, who in the appointed time would have a son to fulfill what God had already predestined.

Listen to verse 11: "For the children being not yet born, neither having done any good or evil that the purpose of God according to election might stand, not of works, but of him that calls."

Then God said in verse 12, the older son shall serve the younger. Then he confirms it by giving an example of Moses and Pharaoh in verses 15-18:

15 For he said to Moses, I will have mercy on whom I will have mercy, and I will have compassion on whom I will have compassion.

16 So then it is not of him that wills, nor of him that runs, but of God that shows mercy.

17 For the scripture says unto Pharaoh, **Even for this same purpose have I raised thee up,** that I might shew my power in thee, and that my name might be declared throughout all the earth.

18 Therefore hath he mercy on whom he will have mercy, and whom he will he hardens.

So God said to Moses, I will have mercy on whom I will have mercy, and compassion on whom I will have compassion. God is basically saying that I can do what I want to do because I am God!

The profoundness of the scripture can be found in verse 17: "Even for this same purpose have I raised thee up that I might shew my power in thee, and that my name might be declared throughout all the earth."

The LORD said these things I have predestined and purposed because I am God, and Pharaoh is an instrument that I will use for my righteous purposes!

Charles Spurgeon said that predestination (election) and free will (choice) are like two parallel lines that don't ever seem to touch. But he said that if you follow them far enough, all the way up to Heaven, they meet each other. This is a very profound statement! In other words it doesn't matter if God predetermined it, or you chose it, it is all for the purposes and glory of God.

Let's read the passage of scripture in Ephesians 1: 3-12. As you read, focus on verses 4, 5, 9 and 11.

Eph 1:3 Blessed be the God and Father of our Lord Jesus Christ, who has blessed us with every spiritual blessing in the heavenly places in Christ,

Eph 1:4 just as He chose us in Him before the foundation of the world, that we should be holy and without blame before Him in love,

Eph 1:5 having predestined us to adoption as sons by Jesus Christ to Himself, according to the good pleasure of His will,

Eph 1:6 to the praise of the glory of His grace, by which He made us accepted in the Beloved.

Eph 1:7 In Him we have redemption through His blood, the forgiveness of sins, according to the riches of His grace

Eph 1:8 which He made to abound toward us in all wisdom and prudence,

Eph 1:9 having made known to us the mystery of His will, according to His good pleasure which He purposed in Himself,

Eph 1:10 that in the dispensation of the fullness of the times He might gather together in one all things in Christ, both which are in heaven and which are on earth—in Him.

Eph 1:11 In Him also we have obtained an inheritance, being predestined according to the purpose of Him who works all things according to the counsel of His will,

Eph 1:12 that we who first trusted in Christ should be to the praise of His glory.

When we look verses 4, 5, 9 and 11, they all speak of predestination. So Paul says, God has chosen us in

Him before the foundations of the world, and predestined us as Sons in Jesus Christ according to the good pleasure of His will. He has also made known to us the mystery of His will according to His good pleasure, which He purposed in Himself. We have also obtained an inheritance, being predestined according to the purpose of Him who works all things according to the counsel of His will.

Child of God, this is profound! Paul is saying that according to the divine purpose of God, we have been predestined and chosen according to God's own purpose and his perfect will! Which means that although we have chosen and made decisions that affect your lives and future, God has already predestined it according to his own purpose and will.

This is why the Apostle Paul said in Romans 8:30-31
30 Moreover whom he did predestinate, them he also called: and whom he called, them he also justified: and whom he justified, them he also glorified.
31 What shall we then say to these things? If God be for us, who can be against us?

Paul is literally saying that if God predestinated, called, justified and glorified us, then he has already worked it out for our good and his glory. In other words God is in control! This should encourage you! Child of God, be encouraged and know that "If God be for you, who can be against you! To God be the glory for his blessed Word!

CHAPTER 3

PURPOSE

"And we know that all things work together for good
to those who love God, to those who are the called
according to His purpose."
Romans 8:28 NKJV

One of the things that every human being has been
endowed with is purpose. I have not met one person
who at some point in their life has not thought about
their purpose! This is one of the great questions of
mankind! Why am I here? What am I supposed to
do? What have I been called to do? Could it be that
God placed purpose in our hearts and minds when
we were in our mother's womb?

There is a scripture in the book of Jeremiah chapter
1:4-5 that speaks volumes as it relates to purpose.
Let's take a look!

"Then the word of the LORD came to me, saying:
"Before I formed you in the womb I knew you; before
you were born I sanctified you; I ordained you a
prophet to the nations."
Jeremiah 1:4-5 NKJV

Throughout the Bible we find God using ordinary
people like you and me to fulfill his purposes in the
earth. When you think about all of the inventions,

books, and things that have been created in the world, we need to know that it all came from God.

In the book of Exodus, God calls and gives Moses the Ten Commandments and the blueprint for the Tabernacle. Moses then begins to share with the people all that God put in his heart to construct the Tabernacle, where God would dwell among his people. The powerful thing about God meeting with Moses is that God gives him a divine blueprint that came from heaven. He also endowed individuals with creative gifts to work with Moses and to assist in the construction of it.

Exodus 35:30-35 NKJV
30 And Moses said to the children of Israel, "See, the LORD has called by name Bezalel the son of Uri, the son of Hur, of the tribe of Judah;
31 and He has filled him with the Spirit of God, in wisdom and understanding, in knowledge and all manner of workmanship,
32 to design artistic works, to work in gold and silver and bronze,
33 in cutting jewels for setting, in carving wood, and to work in all manner of artistic workmanship.
34 "And He has put in his heart the ability to teach, in him and Aholiab the son of Ahisamach, of the tribe of Dan.
35 He has filled them with skill to do all manner of work of the engraver and the designer and the tapestry maker, in blue, purple, and scarlet thread,

and fine linen, and of the weaver—those who do every work and those who design artistic works.

Isn't it amazing that God gives Moses the blueprint for the tabernacle and equips these gifted men with the ability to assist Moses. The powerful thing about these men is that they had divine purpose! Do you not know that every gift, talent and ability that you have came from God?

The Bible says in the book of James chapter 1, verse 17, "Every good and perfect gift comes down from the Father of heavenly lights." God is the giver of all good gifts and great things. He has given us the solar system and earth systems to sustain us. He has created the human body with systems that sustain life. God has created everything in this earth with a divine purpose system!

As a matter of fact, right where you are, take a look at the chair you are sitting in, the desk that you are sitting at, the computer that you are using, and the car that you drive. It has a purpose! Everything has a purpose. There is nothing in this earth that does not have a purpose. So if everything you have in your possession has a purpose, wouldn't it make perfect common sense to say that everything in the earth that God created, has been divinely created with a purpose in mind? The Bible says in Psalms 24:1-2:

1 A Psalm of David. The earth is the LORD's, and all its fullness, the world and those who dwell therein.

2 For He has founded it upon the seas, and established it upon the waters.

In other words, everything that exists in the earth belongs to the LORD, and he has established it for his good pleasure and purpose. This is confirmed in the book of Isaiah where the LORD says in Isaiah 46:10-11:

"Declaring the end from the beginning, and from ancient times the things that are not yet done, saying, My counsel shall stand, and I will do all my pleasure: Calling a ravenous bird from the east, the man that executes my counsel from a far country: yea, I have spoken it, I will also bring it to pass; I have purposed it, I will also do it." Isaiah 46:10-11 KJV

This is a very profound passage of scripture spoken by the LORD through the Prophet Isaiah. The LORD said I declare the end from the beginning. This speaks of predestation, or in other words, that which God has preordained for his purpose!

He even says that my counsel will stand, and I will do all my pleasure. I will even raise up a bird, or a human being to execute my counsel and will. Did you know that God can use anything to achieve his sovereign purposes in the earth?

We find in the Bible that this actually happened. In the story of Elijah the Prophet found in 1 Kings 17, we find after the LORD prophesied that there would be a drought and no rain, and he gave Elijah a Word in

1 Kings 17:2-6:

2 And the word of the LORD came unto him, saying,
3 Get thee hence, and turn thee eastward, and hide
thyself by the brook Cherith, that is before Jordan.
4 And it shall be that thou shalt drink of the brook;
and I have commanded the ravens to feed thee there.
5 So he went and did according unto the word of the
LORD: for he went and dwelt by the brook Cherith,
that is before Jordan.
6 And the ravens brought him bread and flesh in the
morning, and bread and flesh in the evening; and he
drank of the brook.

Did you hear that? As God gives Elijah instructions to
go to a particular place, he raised up a ravenous bird
to fulfill a purpose. The raven is a scavenger by
nature, but it brought food to Elijah in the morning
and evening. In other words God provided for the
man of God despite the drought and lack of water.
God provided just as he said he would, and used a
bird to fulfill his purpose!

God said in Isaiah 46:11, "Yes I will bring it to pass; I
have purposed it and I will do it!" Wow! What a
passage of scripture! We must also understand that
time and season is the measuring rod for anything to
come to pass when God ordains it for a specific
purpose. So let us always remember that delayed
does not mean denied!

Earlier in the chapter, I said that nothing happens by accident but by divine ordination of the Lord.
In theology we said that there are two schools of thought as it relates to God's Divine Purpose and they are:

1.   Predestination or election.
2.   Free will.

Predestination or election states that God has chosen or ordained everything in the earth, and it shall come to pass as he has declared it to be. Freewill says that my destiny and future, are determined by the decisions I make, and the steps I take.

There are some things that God has specifically ordained and elected to come to pass according to his Word. Yet, we as human beings still have a will and a mind to make a choice with decisions that govern our lives! This is important as well, because God did not create us to be robots. We have a will to do, or not to do, and to be, or not to be, this is the answer to be quite specific!

For example, many of you are reading this book because you made a decision to do it, that's freewill! But predestination says, it was ordained that you would buy it and be reading it today! I believe both of these are correct, because there is a purpose why you are reading this, and there is something that God wants you to hear, encourage and empower you for your purpose.

You need to know, my brother and sister, when you accepted Jesus Christ as Lord and Savior, it started a chain of events in your life that have led you to where you are today!

There is one important point I have to make. I have found that you can only find your true purpose in Jesus Christ. I don't say this lightly, because truth be told I was raised in the church as a child, but as I got older, I did not want to be a Christian or to serve the LORD. Yet somehow, through a chain of events ordained and purposed by God, I got back on the right track. I confessed and repented of my sins, recommitted my life to the LORD, was baptized, and God has used me to encourage, strengthen, mentor and bring many people to salvation in Jesus Christ!

Everything that you have been through in life has been part of the journey no matter how good or bad it has been! True purpose is not found in anything except for what God ordains! You cannot find true purpose in money, a man, a woman, or education, although these things can add to your purpose in the right intention!

True purpose can only come from the originator or creator. If you want to find the purpose of a thing, go back to the manufacturer! So what is purpose? The late Myles Munroe said, "Purpose is the original intent for the creation of a thing. The original reason for the existence of a thing, and the cause for the creation of a thing. Purpose, therefore is the original intent in the mind of the originator, or creator that motivated him to create a particular thing for a particular use."

Today the Lord has a Word for each and every one of us, because we all have a purpose, not just any purpose, but a divine purpose that God ordained before the foundations of the earth. Let's look at Ephesian 1:9-11. This is a profound chapter in Ephesians. Look at the language and words Paul uses very carefully as he describes God's divine purpose system in Christ for your life.

Ephesians 1:9-11 KJV
9 Having made known unto us the mystery of his will, **according to his good pleasure which he has purposed in himself:**
10 That in the dispensation of the fullness of times he might gather together in one all things in Christ, both which are in heaven, and which are on earth; even in him:
11 In whom also we have obtained an inheritance, being predestinated **according to the purpose of him who works all things after the counsel of his own will.**

The Apostle Paul in his letter to the Ephesians uses some language that is very profound as it relates to purpose. Look at verse 9:

9 Having made known unto us the mystery of his will, **according to his good pleasure which he hath purposed in himself:**

10 That in the dispensation of the fullness of times he might gather together in one all things in Christ, both which are in heaven, and which are on earth; even in him:

11 In whom also we have obtained an inheritance, being predestinated **according to the purpose of him who works all things after the counsel of his own will.**

Notice that the scripture says that he purposed it according to his good pleasure. It also says in verse 11, that we have obtained an inheritance being predestinated according to the purpose of him who works all things after the counsel of his own will.

Everything that God has purposed has been done according to the good pleasure of his will, the mystery of his will, and the counsel after his own will. This means that everything that we are walking out now as it relates to purpose is because God has done it according to his own sovereign will!

Jesus Understood His Purpose

When we look at scripture, we find that Jesus understood his purpose and would not let anyone or anything stop him from divine purpose. There are many people in the body of Christ who have allowed people, situations, circumstances and even the devil to distract them from their purpose. As we can see from scripture, the Lord would not be distracted from his purpose.

Matthew 16:21-23 NKJV
21 From that time Jesus began to show to His disciples that He must go to Jerusalem, and suffer many things from the elders and chief priests and scribes, and be killed, and be raised the third day.
22 Then Peter took Him aside and began to rebuke Him, saying, "Far be it from You, Lord; this shall not happen to You!"
23 But He turned and said to Peter, "Get behind Me, Satan! You are an offense to Me, for you are not mindful of the things of God, but the things of men."

As we see, Peter thought that he was doing a great thing by trying to save Jesus life, and to keep him from going to the cross. Jesus would have no part of what Peter wanted to do. He knew that it was not Peter, but the spirit of the evil one attempting to work through Peter. In other words, Jesus said, "I know why I am here, and what my Father has called me to do." In other words, I understand my purpose!

John said the following about Jesus "He who sins is of the devil, for the devil has sinned from the beginning. For this purpose the Son of God was manifested, that He might destroy the works of the devil."
1 John 3:8 NKJV

When we read these scriptures we find that Jesus definitely understood his assignment and purpose while he was on earth. There are a lot of people on earth today that are willing to compromise their God given purpose for comfort, money, fame and fortune. When you study the life of Jesus Christ, he would not be deterred from his purpose. He knew that he was the Son of God, and had a purpose to fulfill.

Jesus knew that the world needed salvation, and had to be delivered from the power of Satan. Jesus fulfilled purpose by going to the cross, shedding his blood, being resurrected from the dead, and delivered us from the curse of the law of sin and death. That was his purpose! So the question today is what is your purpose? What have you been birthed into the earth to fulfill and accomplish in Jesus Christ?

I have found that personal fulfillment in life comes from a purposed filled life and destiny in Christ! You can certainly fulfill purpose in life, but the LORD gives you divine purpose! We must always remember that there is a difference!

Called According to God's Purpose

Many years ago I had the opportunity to meet an anointed man of God who wrote many books on the Kingdom of God, faith, vision and purpose. He went home to be with the LORD many years ago, but the impact he made on the Body of Christ was a great blessing!

I can recall him saying the following about purpose:

"The greatest tragedy in life is not death, but life without a reason. It is dangerous to be alive and not know why you were given life. Our young generation today seems to have lost direction and purpose."
-Myles Munroe

It is amazing that God who is able to do all things uses human vessels to fulfill his divine purposes in the earth! How many of us know that God can use anything at his disposal. Listen to the Apostle Paul!

2 Timothy 1:8-9 NKJV
8 Therefore do not be ashamed of the testimony of our Lord, nor of me His prisoner, but share with me in the sufferings for the gospel according to the power of God,
9 who has saved us and called us with a holy calling, not according to our works, but according to His own purpose, and grace which was given to us in Christ Jesus before time began.

The scripture states that God has saved us and called us with a holy calling, not according to our works, but according to the LORD's own purpose and grace, which was given to us in Christ Jesus before time began.

This scripture implies that God not only saved and called us, but he did it according to his own divine purpose, even before time began. In other words God has predestined and purposed some things for you and me for our good and for his glory.

So the question is, "Are you fulfilling your purpose? This is why being in the perfect will of God is so important, because when we are in his perfect will, we are under his divine protection in the midst of trials, tribulations, troubles, tests and temptations of life! Being in the God's will does not mean we are exempt from them, but he will keep us through the fire and the storms of life.

This is why we need to endeavor to be in the perfect will of God! Because in his perfect will is provision and protection as you journey toward your purpose in Christ! But the key thing to remember is "Obedience, Faith and Humility."

Also remember if you get out of the will of God, you are headed for a detour. A detour is a rerouted road to your destination! Many of us understand that a detour is when construction on a road is being performed and you are rerouted. Some of us have experienced what it means to be on a detour in life, and someone reading this book may be on one right now.

What is a detour? It is a rerouted route to get to a specific destination because construction is going on.

Many of God's people are under construction for purpose. If you get out of the will of God, you are headed for a detour until the work in you is complete.

The LORD showed me that sometimes people will make decisions that are out of the will of God, but because of purpose, God will take them on a detour to get them to purpose.

Remember the children of Israel? God's hand was upon the nation of Israel, and they were journeying to the Promised Land of purpose. But because of murmuring, complaining, disobedience and idolatry they stayed in the wilderness longer than they should have. Some theologians say that the journey should have taken weeks, but they ended up in the desert for 40 years.

Even in ministry, instead of doing the will of God, we do our own will, which can cause us to be out of the perfect will of God. Believe me I have made decisions in life based on my own will and paid the price! But because of God's grace and purpose for my life, I went on a detour and was rerouted to my purpose and destiny. I finally got there, but what if I had been more patience and waited on the LORD?

People leave churches far earlier than what God planned because of the wrong reason. I guarantee they will be on a detour until they repent and get back on the right track to purpose and destiny!

That's why David wrote a profound Psalm in Psalm 91 about abiding and taking refuge in the presence of God, and why it is the safest place to be!

Psalms 91:1-2 KJV
1 He that dwelleth in the secret place of the Most High shall abide under the shadow of the Almighty.
2 I will say of the LORD, He is my refuge and my fortress: my God; in him will I trust.

When you have a purpose, nothing should stop you from doing what the LORD called you to do. The most important thing to do is have the right attitude, stay in prayer, stay in the presence of God and above all, stay in the Word of God!

I have found that when you truly find your purpose you find peace for your life. Your peace is found in a life full of purpose. One of the cravings of the human spirit is to find relevance and reason for existence. The fact that you are alive and still in the land of the living is evidence that God has something in store for your life.

Even in the church, people get comfortable and start just going through the motions. God never intended for us to just walk by faith, but to put our faith into action. There are 4 important points that you need to remember that will help you fulfill your purpose.

1. Purpose for your life is determined by God.

We were designed by the hands of God to have a

meaningful purpose. You will never find your purpose outside of a relationship with Jesus Christ. Jesus said, "I am the way, the truth and the life." (John 14:6) If you want to discover God's will for your life. The first step is to surrender completely to the LORD.

You find truth for your existence in Jesus Christ. Some people contact psychics for direction, some people consult the zodiacs signs for direction and purpose, but these are all false prophets, who can never give you true purpose. You want to find your purpose, consult the Creator of the heavens and earth. Why because he made you?

As a matter of fact when you want to find how to operate a piece of machinery, or put something together. What do you do? You consult the instructions or the company that made the product who will assist you! As a matter of fact when you buy something online, many times the creator or manufacturer of the product will send you an email, stating that if you have problems with the product, contact this person or number.

Isn't this what he should be doing as it relates to our life and purpose in Christ? I remember a Pastor once asked me, "What's the difference between a psychic and prophet? He answered, "A psychic tells you what's on your mind; a prophet tells you what's on God's mind." A psychic see it, but a prophet can change it.

Jesus endured the pain of the cross because he knew he had a purpose. When you have purpose, you don't run, hide or try to make a way out of your way. You let God have his way and he will make a way.

How would it feel to work hard all of your life and fulfill nothing? When you live your life with purpose, it doesn't matter how much money you have, how your situation looks, or whatever troubles you may have, because God will give you divine direction for our purpose!

2. Purpose will make your life easier to understand.

When you have purpose, there is nothing that can stop you from doing the perfect will of God. Purpose gives you understanding despite everything you may be going through or experienced in life. The Apostle Paul said something so profound in one of the most beloved and quoted scriptures in the Bible.

Romans 8:28 NKJV
28 And we know that all things work together for good to those who love God, to those who are the called according to His purpose. The Word of God says that all things will work together for good to those who love God, who are called according to his purpose. In other words, no matter what it looks like, or appears to be, God's purpose will prevail in your life for the good.

3. Purpose hopes for tomorrow.

When you understand purpose, you have a hope and an expectation for God to do something awesome and great in your life. Why? Because dreams and visions give hope for tomorrow. A life without purpose lives for the now, and never dreams or hopes for tomorrow. If what you are doing today is the same thing you did yesterday and there is no fulfillment, then you need to reevaluate your life and make some changes.

Many people desire to be remembered here on earth when they die. But you will never be remembered without fulfilling your divine purpose. You were born to fulfill a purpose and your purpose is defined by God. Only the divine purpose of God in your life can give you fulfillment and cause you to leave a lasting legacy.

Child of God, you have something in you that is waiting to be exhaled into your family, your community and everybody that you come in contact with. But you must make the right choices! Spirit led choices provide the path that opens the doors to our destiny. Decisions out of the will of God can have devastating results. Judas had purpose, but the wrong choices which eventually took his life. Samson had purpose, but he made the wrong decisions that eventually took his life. King Saul had purpose, but he made the wrong decisions that eventually took his life. When God gives you purpose, there is hope for tomorrow that the vision, dreams and goals that encompasses your life will propel you into purpose.

CHAPTER 4

PLANS

"A man's heart devises his way: but the
LORD directs his steps."
Proverbs 16:9 KJV

When we read the book of Proverbs we find so much wisdom as it relates to our lives. We stated in earlier chapters that God has given us freewill but the wisdom of Prov 16:9 says that although we devise or plan our way, the LORD directs our steps.

When we look at Prov 16:9 in other translations we find the word plans instead of devise. Both words are used in relation to a person making decisions, setting goals, and planning his way. There are other translations that use the word plans.

"A man's heart plans his way, but Jehovah directs his steps." MKJV

"We can make many plans, but the LORD determines our steps." NLT

The word devise in the Hebrew is khaw-shab' from the *Strong's Talking Greek & Hebrew Dictionary* which means to plot or contrive, to think, regard, value, compute, conceive, consider, count, devise, esteem, or imagine.
In other words God has given us the freewill to plan, devise, and consider but God will direct our steps. As it relates to the divine purpose of God in our lives, this is important.

Is there anyone reading this that can testify that although we make plans, sometimes it doesn't always go according to what we plan.

I can testify that 90% of the time, whatever I plan and dream up in my own mind, never fully comes to pass as I thought it would. But for some reason it always works out for the good. Could this be what the Psalmist is saying in regards to a man's way? We devise plans, but God said I direct your steps.

This is a powerful scripture because we see freewill and predestination working together. We devise and plan, but God directs our steps! To be truthful, this is good because although we understand the importance of writing a vision, planning and strategizing as it relates to goals, dreams, and aspirations, God orders our steps.

I am so glad that God orders our steps because as human beings we have the potential to do something out of the will of God, and we have the potential to do something out of season because of impatience. So the LORD said I will direct your steps. There is another scripture that confirms this in Prov 19:21.

"There are many devices in a man's heart; nevertheless the counsel of the LORD, that shall stand." Proverbs 19:21 KJV

It says that although we have many plans in our heart, the counsel of the LORD that shall stand. As we read this scripture we see the importance of being in the perfect will of God as it relates to purpose. I don't know about you, but I want my plans to line up with the divine purpose of God for my life.

Many times we plan and make decisions for our lives because it is a good idea, or something we think would be good to do. The scripture admonishes us in Prov 3:5-6, "To trust in the LORD with all of our heart, and to lean not to our own understanding, but in all of our ways, acknowledge the LORD and he will direct our paths."

Earlier in the book we looked at Jesus in the Garden of Gethsemane which can be found in Matt 26. In this chapter we find a profound example of Christ submitting his will to the will of the Father. We also find that Christ expressed his desire to let this cup (going to the cross) pass him by, but he allowed the will of the Father to direct his steps. Let's read!

Matthew 26:39-42 NKJV
39 He went a little farther and fell on His face, and prayed, saying, "O My Father, if it is possible, let this cup pass from Me; nevertheless, not as I will, but as You will."
40 Then He came to the disciples and found them sleeping, and said to Peter, "What! Could you not watch with Me one hour?
41 Watch and pray, lest you enter into temptation. The spirit indeed is willing, but the flesh is weak."
42 Again, a second time, He went away and prayed, saying, "O My Father, if this cup cannot pass away from Me unless I drink it, Your will be done."

Let us understand that Jesus was the Son of God, but was also the Son of Man. Christ knew the weight of sin and pain that would be experienced at the cross was a heavy task and weight for anyone to accomplish. This was not disobedience to the purpose or plan of God, it was Christ communing with the Father the pain and sorrow that was about to take place by dying at the cross.

He did what any human being would do at that hour by saying, "Father if it be possible let this cup pass from me. Nevertheless, not as I will, but as you will."

The Bible says there are many plans in a man's heart, but it is the LORD's purpose, or his counsel that will stand! Christ shows us the ultimate example as it relates to the plan of God for our lives. We must submit our will to his will, and our plans to his plans.

Why because as the LORD told Jeremiah in Jer 29:11, "For I know the thoughts that I think toward you, says the LORD, thoughts of peace and not of evil, to give you a future and a hope."

Child of God, although the plan of God may seem out of place and painful, his plans are perfect and there is a greater purpose that God desires to fulfill!

When Christ gave his life as a sacrifice for the sins of the world, he took the weight of sin upon himself when he shed his blood, died and was resurrected on the third day. As a result we have everlasting life! Christ death at the cross was the Fathers plan of salvation for every human being on this planet. Likewise, we should submit ourselves to God's plan for our life which is always for our good and his glory.

CHAPTER 5

PROMISES

"And if you are Christ's, then you are Abraham's
seed, and heirs according to the promise."
Galatians 3:29 NKJV

The Apostle Paul said if we are Christ's, then we
are Abraham's seed, and heirs according to the
promise. This is a powerful passage of scripture. So
when we think about the promises of God, what
comes to your mind? I could ask five believers this
question and I am sure I would get some interesting
answers.

So what is a promise? "It is an assurance that
something will or will not happen, or a pledge to do
or not do something. It is a covenant, and it also
provides a basis for expectation." There are so many
promises that have been made to us in the Bible
especially for the obedient believer, but you will only
lay hold of those promises by faith. We find that God
made many promises to the people of God. God made
a covenant with Noah in Genesis 6: 18. In Genesis
chapter 6:5-18, the earth had become full of violence
and corrupt. Noah was a righteous man and Gen 6:8
says, "But Noah found grace in the eyes of the LORD"
and a promise was made to him.

Genesis 6:17-18 NKJV
17 And behold, I Myself am bringing floodwaters on
the earth, to destroy from under heaven all flesh in
which is the breath of life; everything that is on the
earth shall die.

18 But I will establish My covenant with you; and you shall go into the ark—you, your sons, your wife, and your sons' wives with you.

The promise or covenant was given to Noah and his family to protect them as God rendered judgment upon the earth.

We all know the story. It rained forty days and forty nights upon the earth, but God protected Noah and his family. We then find that God confirmed the covenant agreement or promise with him.

Gen 9:8 Then God spoke to Noah and to his sons with him, saying:
Gen 9:9 And as for Me, behold, I establish My covenant with you and with your descendants after you,
Gen 9:10 and with every living creature that is with you: the birds, the cattle, and every beast of the earth with you, of all that go out of the ark, every beast of the earth.
Gen 9:11 Thus I establish My covenant with you: Never again shall all flesh be cut off by the waters of the flood; never again shall there be a flood to destroy the earth."
Gen 9:12 And God said: "This is the sign of the covenant which I make between Me and you, and every living creature that is with you, for perpetual generations:
Gen 9:13 I set My rainbow in the cloud, and it shall be for the sign of the covenant between Me and the earth.
Gen 9:14 It shall be, when I bring a cloud over the earth, that the rainbow shall be seen in the cloud;

Gen 9:15 and I will remember my covenant which is between Me and you and every living creature of all flesh; the waters shall never again become a flood to destroy all flesh.

Gen 9:16 The rainbow shall be in the cloud, and I will look on it to remember the everlasting covenant between God and every living creature of all flesh that is on the earth."

Gen 9:17 And God said to Noah, "This is the sign of the covenant which I have established between me and all flesh that is on the earth."

Abraham was also given a promise and a covenant that was confirmed many times in scripture.

Genesis 12:1-4 NKJV
1 Now the LORD had said to Abram: "Get out of your country, from your family and from your father's house, To a land that I will show you.
2 I will make you a great nation; I will bless you and make your name great; and you shall be a blessing.
3 I will bless those who bless you, and I will curse him who curses you; and in you all the families of the earth shall be blessed."
4 So Abram departed as the LORD had spoken to him, and Lot went with him. And Abram was seventy-five years old when he departed from Haran.

Genesis 13:14-17 NKJV
14 And the LORD said to Abram, after Lot had separated from him: "Lift your eyes now and look from the place where you are—northward, southward, eastward, and westward;
15 for all the land which you see I give to you and your descendants forever.

16 And I will make your descendants as the dust of the earth; so that if a man could number the dust of the earth, then your descendants also could be numbered.

17 Arise, walk in the land through its length and its width, for I give it to you."

Gen 17:1 When Abram was ninety-nine years old, the LORD appeared to Abram and said to him, "I am Almighty God; walk before Me and be blameless.

Gen 17:2 And I will make my covenant between Me and you, and will multiply you exceedingly."

Gen 17:3 Then Abram fell on his face, and God talked with him, saying:

Gen 17:4 As for Me, behold, my covenant is with you, and you shall be a father of many nations.

Gen 17:5 No longer shall your name be called Abram, but your name shall be Abraham; for I have made you a father of many nations.

Gen 17:6 I will make you exceedingly fruitful; and I will make nations of you, and kings shall come from you.

Gen 17:7 And I will establish My covenant between Me and you and your descendants after you in their generations, for an everlasting covenant, to be God to you and your descendants after you.

Gen 17:8 Also I give to you and your descendants after you the land in which you are a stranger, all the land of Canaan, as an everlasting possession; and I will be their God."

Gen 17:9 And God said to Abraham: "As for you, you shall keep My covenant, you and your descendants after you throughout their generations.

The covenant promises of God made to Abraham were fulfilled through his obedience!

Genesis 22:15-18 NKJV
15 Then the Angel of the LORD called to Abraham a second time out of heaven,
16 and said: "By Myself I have sworn, says the LORD, because you have done this thing, and have not withheld your son, your only son—
17 blessing I will bless you, and multiplying I will multiply your descendants as the stars of the heaven and as the sand which is on the seashore; and your descendants shall possess the gate of their enemies.
18 In your seed all the nations of the earth shall be blessed, because you have obeyed my voice."

The children of Israel were given many promises based on their obedience.

Deuteronomy 26:16-19 NKJV
16 This day the LORD your God commands you to observe these statutes and judgments; therefore you shall be careful to observe them with all your heart and with all your soul.
17 Today you have proclaimed the LORD to be your God, and that you will walk in His ways and keep His statutes, His commandments, and His judgments, and that you will obey His voice.
18 Also today the LORD has proclaimed you to be His special people, just as He promised you, that you should keep all His commandments,
19 and that He will set you high above all nations which He has made, in praise, in name, and in honor, and that you may be a holy people to the LORD your God, just as He has spoken.

The Promised Land was one of many promises that God made to the children of Israel. Only two out twelve men and their families, and those under the age of twenty one entered in. The rest did not enter in because of their disobedience and unbelief.

Numbers 14:22-24 NKJV
22 because all these men who have seen My glory and the signs which I did in Egypt and in the wilderness, and have put Me to the test now these ten times, and have not heeded My voice,
23 they certainly shall not see the land of which I swore to their fathers, nor shall any of those who rejected me see it.
24 But My servant Caleb, because he has a different spirit in him and has followed me fully, I will bring into the land where he went, and his descendants shall inherit it.

It is very important to know what the Word of God says concerning the promises of God, because you can then know what to expect, and it gives us hope for the future. The promises made to Abraham ultimately related to Jesus Christ. It was a promise that in him all would be blessed.

Abraham believed God and received the promise of God for his faith. If you are a born again believer in Christ who has been born of his spirit and washed in his blood you are the spiritual descendants of Abraham and the promises of God belong to you. The Bible gives us scripture about what God has prepared and promised for us in his Word when we receive it by faith. Let's take a look at some scriptures in Galatians 3.

Galatians 3:5-9 NKJV

5 Therefore He who supplies the Spirit to you and works miracles among you, does He do it by the works of the law, or by the hearing of faith?

6 just as Abraham "Believed God, and it was accounted to him for righteousness."

7 Therefore know that only those who are of faith are sons of Abraham.

8 And the Scripture, foreseeing that God would justify the Gentiles by faith, preached the gospel to Abraham beforehand, saying, "In you all the nations shall be blessed."

9 So then those who are of faith are blessed with believing Abraham.

The Apostle Paul shares with us in these passages of scripture that miracles that are worked among us come by faith and not by the law. He also says that Abraham believed God and it was accounted unto him as righteousness. The Bible says that Abraham received a covenant promise from God through his obedience, and as a result God blessed him and his descendants.

Gen 22:18 "In your seed all the nations of the earth shall be blessed, because you have obeyed My voice."

Paul then says that we who believe by faith are also blessed with believing Abraham. Paul does not stop there, he then goes on to say that we are all sons of God through faith in Christ Jesus! Each and every one of us who have been baptized in the name of Jesus Christ and born again have put on Christ! It does not matter whether we are male, female, Jew, Greek, Black, White, Asian, Hispanic, or Indian!

We are all one in Jesus Christ, and we are heirs according to the promise!

Galatians 3:26-29 NKJV
26 For you are all sons of God through faith in Christ Jesus.
27 For as many of you as were baptized into Christ have put on Christ.
28 There is neither Jew nor Greek, there is neither slave nor free, there is neither male nor female; for you are all one in Christ Jesus.
29 And if you are Christ's, then you are Abraham's seed, and heirs according to the promise.

The Bible says that we are heirs according to the promise. What is an heir?

1. A person who inherits or is entitled by law or by the terms of a will to inherit the estate of another.
2. A person who succeeds or is in line to succeed to a hereditary rank, title, or office.
3. One who receives or is expected to receive a heritage from a predecessor or a person who is before them and leaves them an inheritance.

The Bible says in Gal 3:29, "And if you are Christ's, then you are Abraham's seed, and heirs according to the promise."

Now when we talk about an heir we are speaking of someone in our family line or genealogy. Look what the Bible says about genealogy!

Mat 1:1 "The book of the generation of Jesus Christ, the son of David, the son of Abraham."

Then says in Mat 1:17, "So all the generations from Abraham to David are fourteen generations; and from David until the carrying away into Babylon are fourteen generations; and from the carrying away into Babylon unto Christ are fourteen generations."

The Apostle Paul said in Gal 3:29, "And if you are Christ's, then you are Abraham's seed, and heirs according to the promise."

This means that you and I are partakers of the covenant promises made to Father Abraham!

Now there are so many promises that have been made to us in the Bible because of our salvation in Christ. We need to know all the promises we have in Christ, and it all starts when we believe, receive and accept Jesus Christ as LORD and Savior according to Romans 10:9. Receiving the covenant promises of God made to Abraham are predicated on our acceptance of salvation in Jesus Christ! Everything else is a secondary to it! Salvation in the Greek is the word: sōtēria "so-tay-ree'-ah" which means rescue or safety (physically or morally): Deliver, health, salvation, and to save.

When we understand and accept this first promise that comes through salvation, then we have access to all others! When we receive salvation in Christ there are promises concerning peace, power, protection, provision and prosperity. Let's take a look at some of those promises!

Peace

"You will keep him in perfect peace, whose mind is stayed on you, because he trusts in you."
Isaiah 26:3 NKJV

There are many believers that don't have peace of mind. They are worried, they have fear, and they are concerned with so many things in the world. The truth of the matter is if you are discouraged, dismayed or depressed, God has given us peace through the Prince of Peace; Jesus Christ.

Although I am the bearer of good news which is the Gospel, I have some bad news! There will never be true peace on this earth until the Prince of Peace; Jesus Christ returns. Before Christ returns, the Anti-Christ will arise and bring forth peace, but it will be false peace.

This is why our minds should be stayed on Jesus Christ, because he will keep us in perfect peace as we trust in him.

What is peace?
1. Peace is a state of quiet or tranquility; freedom from disturbance or agitation.
2. Freedom from internal commotion or civil war.
3. Freedom from private or public quarrels, suits or disturbance.
4. Freedom from agitation or disturbance by the passions, as from fear, terror, anger, anxiety or the like; quietness of mind; tranquility; calmness; quiet of conscience.

How many of know that when you repented of your sins, and accepted Jesus Christ as Lord and Savior, peace was restored between you and God? In other words peace was imparted into your spirit, soul and mind. A person that has not accepted Jesus Christ as LORD and Savior, and who is in sin has not made peace with God.

Joh 16:33 says, "These things I have spoken to you, that in Me you may have peace. In the world you will have tribulation; but be of good cheer, I have overcome the world."

Jesus said in the world you will have tribulation, but in me you will have peace! This is why we must keep our minds stayed on the LORD! What has enabled many believers in the midst of many trials and tribulations to have peace is to keep their minds stayed on Jesus! It is our relationship with him that enables us to have peace in this world!

Somewhere along the line, the enemy has deceived many people and stolen their peace of mind, and faith in Jesus Christ. So we find many people trusting in the arm of flesh instead of trusting in the LORD, and walking in complete faith.

Now remember I said that when God saved us, peace was imparted into our spirit, soul and mind. That's why it is so important to be filled with the Holy Spirit. The Bible says when Jesus was baptized, the heavens were opened, and the Holy Spirit descended on him like a dove in Luke 3:21-22 NKJV.

21 When all the people were baptized, it came to pass that Jesus also was baptized; and while He prayed, the heaven was opened.

22 And the Holy Spirit descended in bodily form like a dove upon Him, and a voice came from heaven which said, "You are My beloved Son; in You I am well pleased."

 Did you know that the Dove is a symbol of peace? Webster's dictionary defines the Dove as an advocate of peace or of a peaceful policy.

When we have the Holy Spirit we have peace, which is the fruit of the spirit. One of the names for the Lord in the Old Testament is Jehovah Shalom. It means, "The LORD is Peace" Where does the word Jehovah Shalom come from, and where is it found? There are many references to peace in the Bible, but the first place Jehovah Shalom it is found is in the book Judges:

Judges 6:23-24 NKJV
23 Then the LORD said to him, "Peace be with you; do not fear, you shall not die."
24 So Gideon built an altar there to the LORD, and called it **The-LORD-Is-Peace.** To this day it is still in Ophrah of the Abiezrites.

Listen to the context of the scripture. The LORD told Gideon, "Peace be with you, do not fear, you shall not die."

This is so profound. God granted Gideon peace to override his fear, and said you shall not die! This is a profound scripture. Someone reading this needs peace right now, receive it by faith in Jesus Name!

The promise of peace belongs to us as children of God. Being filled with the Holy Spirit brings peace as well. Not only that, but having the LORD on your side in the midst of turmoil is a wonderful thing, because the LORD is peace!

Galatians 5:22-23 NKJV
22 But the fruit of the Spirit is love, joy, peace, longsuffering, kindness, goodness, faithfulness,
23 gentleness, self-control, against such there is no law.

As it relates to peace, the Apostle Paul gives us some great wisdom on being carnally minded and spiritually minded in Romans chapter 8 as well.

Romans 8:5-6 NKJV
5 For those who live according to the flesh set their minds on the things of the flesh, but those who live according to the Spirit, the things of the Spirit.
6 For to be carnally minded is death, but to be spiritually minded is life and peace.

Did you hear that? To be spiritually minded is life and peace, but to be carnally minded is death! Man cannot have real peace until his nature is changed. There is a blessing for the one who walks in and practices peace as well. Matt 5:9 says, "Blessed are the peacemakers: for they shall be called the children of God."

The Bible even says in 1 Cor 14:33, "For God is not the author of confusion but of peace, as in all the churches of the saints."

Keeping your mind stayed on God's Holy word guarantees you peace as well. Psa 119:165 says, "Great peace have those who love your law and nothing causes them to stumble."

When the Word is in your heart and mind, it becomes part of your nature and everyday life. This is why we must keep our minds stayed on Christ in all situations, because he will give us peace of mind!

Isa 26:3 says, "You will keep him in perfect peace, whose mind is stayed on you, because he trusts in you.
Isa 26:4 Trust in the LORD forever, for in YAH, the LORD, is everlasting strength.

God promises in his Word that the righteous or blameless man shall have peace as well.

Psa 37:35 I have seen the wicked in great power, And spreading himself like a native green tree.
Psa 37:36 yet he passed away, and behold, he was no more; Indeed I sought him, but he could not be found.
Psa 37:37 Mark the blameless man, and observe the upright; for the future of that man is peace.

The greatest story about peace comes to us from the book of Mark chapter 4, verses 35-41.

Mark 4:35-41 NKJV
35 On the same day, when evening had come, He said to them, "Let us cross over to the other side."
36 Now when they had left the multitude, they took Him along in the boat as He was, and other little boats were also with Him.

37 And a great windstorm arose, and the waves beat into the boat, so that it was already filling.

38 But He was in the stern, asleep on a pillow. And they awoke Him and said to Him, "Teacher, do You not care that we are perishing?"

39 Then He arose and rebuked the wind, and said to the sea, "Peace, be still!" And the wind ceased and there was a great calm.

40 But He said to them, "Why are you so fearful? How is it that you have no faith?"

41 And they feared exceedingly, and said to one another, "Who can this be? That even the wind and the sea obey Him!"

As we can see Jesus the Prince of Peace was at peace while the windstorm arose and waves beat against the boat. This is an amazing story! While the disciples were hanging on for dear life being tossed to and fro, and water was filling the boat, Jesus was asleep on a pillow.

They then awoke Jesus and said, "Master, or Teacher, Do you care that we are perishing?" In other words, we are about to die and you are asleep! The LORD woke up from a peaceful sleep, and rebuked the wind, and said to the sea, "Peace be still!" The Bible then says that the wind ceased and there was a great calm! We can learn something from this story. Jesus was at peace in the midst of a storm despite the wind and waves beating against the boat. While the disciples were in fear, Jesus was in faith and peace in the boat. People of God, no matter what we go through in life, having the faith of God and the peace of God will enable us to get the victory no matter what we go through in life.

Power

"Behold, I give you power to trample on serpents and
scorpions, and over all the power of the enemy, and
nothing shall by any means hurt you."
Luke 10:19 KJV

One of the most powerful things that Jesus did was
delegate power to the disciples in Luke 10:19 as they
went out sharing the good news of the Kingdom. As
they went forth he gave them power to trample on
serpents and scorpions, and over all the power of the
enemy! In other words he gave them "exousia" in
the Greek which means authority, jurisdiction,
liberty, power, right, and strength. *(Strong's Talking
Greek & Hebrew Dictionary.)*

So although the enemy had power, Jesus said I give
you power over his power, and nothing shall by any
means hurt you! I want you to know that the promise
of power belongs to you and me as well! Because
without the Holy Spirit of God, there is no power for
the believer in Christ!

Acts 1:8 KJV
**8 But ye shall receive power, after that the
Holy Ghost is come upon you: and ye shall be
witnesses unto me both in Jerusalem, and in
all Judaea, and in Samaria, and unto the
uttermost part of the earth.**

In Acts 1:8 we see a different translation for the word
power. The word power in this passage of scripture
comes to us from the Greek word, "dunamis" where
we get the word dynamite, which is an explosive

made from nitroglycerin. Dynamite is used as a weapon or in construction to blow things up, or to destroy a particular thing. Dunamis is defined as; force or miraculous power, might, strength, violence, or mighty work. *(Strong's Talking Greek & Hebrew Dictionary.)*

Power can be natural or supernatural. Power can be used in a good way and a bad way. As believers In Christ, we have the power of the Holy Spirit.

The Apostle Peter who labored alongside Jesus as a disciple had a lot to say about the promise of power as well, because he was a witness of Jesus Christ power!

2 Peter 1:2-4 KJV
2 Grace and peace be multiplied unto you through the knowledge of God, and of Jesus our Lord,
3 According as his divine power hath given unto us all things that pertain unto life and godliness, through the knowledge of him that hath called us to glory and virtue:
4 Whereby are given unto us exceeding great and precious promises: that by these ye might be partakers of the divine nature, having escaped the corruption that is in the world through lust.

Peter said that the LORD's divine power has given us all things that pertain to life and godliness! Not only that but he has given unto us exceeding great and precious promises as well! So in essence we have these precious promises and one of them is divine power for life, and godliness and strength to escape all the corruption that is in the world through lust!

The Apostle Paul also had a lot to say about power. One of my favorite scriptures comes from 2 Tim 1:7.

"For God hath not given us the spirit of fear; but of power, and of love, and of a sound mind."
2 Timothy 1:7 KJV

Paul says that God has not given to us the spirit of fear, why? Because we have the spirit of faith in Jesus Christ our LORD!

He also told Timothy that we must endure hardship as a good soldier in 2 Tim 2:3. I have found in my life that you need faith, power, love and a sound mind to overcome and ensure hardship. Sometimes when we are going through a difficult situation, the spirit of fear comes to discourage us. But we must stand strong by the power of the Holy Spirit!

When you understand the Word of God and the promises of God it will give you the power to stand strong in the midst of adversity. Because when you get knocked down, God will give you the power to get back up! Somebody should encourage themselves right now by saying, I might be down, but I won't stay down in Jesus name!

It is only through the power of God that we are able to get back up and accomplish the purposes of God in the earth. We see all throughout scripture that God empowered individuals to overcome and be victorious by the power of God! There are many examples in scripture of men and women of God who were knocked down in life, but got back up by the power of God!

Moses got back up after killing an Egyptian and going on the run after leaving Egypt. He shepherded sheep for 40 years, then God called him to lead the children of Israel in the wilderness for 40 years toward the Promised Land.

Joseph got back up after being hated on by his brothers, thrown in a pit, sold to slave traders, lied on, thrown in prison, and eventually exonerated and Pharaoh elevated him to 2nd in command in Egypt.

Daniel got back up after refusing to bow down to the King, and was thrown in the lion's den, but the Angel of the LORD protected him. Early the next morning they found Daniel alive with the lions and he came out without a scratch on him.

Samson got back up after Delilah tricked him for the secret to his strength, and God gave him power to destroy the coliseum and the enemy.

David got back up after sinning against God with lust, committing adultery, and murder but ended up being the greatest king in history.

Peter got back up after Jesus called him Satan (Matt 16:21-23), told him to mind his business (John 21:20-22), and he denied the Lord three times. (Matt 26:33-34) Yet, he preached with POWER on the day of Pentecost and 3000 people got saved!

Even Jesus died the death of a transgressor; he was spit on, rejected, beaten like a criminal, crucified, and he died, but after three days, he got up with all POWER in his hand!

I want to encourage you to stand strong in God and understand that the promise of power has been given to you and me! No devil, demon, evil spirit, witch, or warlock has power over the power of Jesus Christ our LORD and Savior, and that power has been delegated to you and me when we believe on his Holy name!

In the book of Ephesians 1 verses 17 -19, Paul prayed for the Ephesians a very profound prayer about power that I believe says it all for you and me. Let's read!

Ephesians 1:15-21 NKJV
15 Therefore I also, after I heard of your faith in the Lord Jesus and your love for all the saints,
16 do not cease to give thanks for you, making mention of you in my prayers:
17 that the God of our Lord Jesus Christ, the Father of glory, may give to you the spirit of wisdom and revelation in the knowledge of Him,
18 the eyes of your understanding being enlightened; that you may know what is the hope of His calling, what are the riches of the glory of His inheritance in the saints,
19 and what is the exceeding greatness of His power toward us who believe, according to the working of His mighty power
20 which He worked in Christ when He raised Him from the dead and seated Him at His right hand in the heavenly places,
21 far above all principality, power, might and dominion, and every name that is named, not only in this age but also in that which is to come.

The Apostle Paul prayed that God would give the saints wisdom, revelation, and knowledge, and that they would understand the exceeding greatness of his power toward those who believe according to his mighty power! Saints of God, you and I have been given dunamis power, miraculous power, and yoke destroying power in the Name of Jesus Christ our LORD! Why because of your faith and believing on his Most High Name!

This is so profound, because it is my prayer that you would understand this power, and walk it out by faith in Jesus Name. We must never forget that we have exceeding great power from on high through the power of the Holy Spirit in Jesus Christ our LORD!

Prosperity

"Beloved, I wish above all things that you may
prosper and be in health, even as your soul prospers."
3 John 1:2 KJV

As we continue our teaching on God's Divine
Purpose System, we see that the promises of God are
very important and belong to you and me! In today's
church we have heard a lot about prosperity. I am
not here to judge or preach against anyone, but what
I want to do is give you clear understanding from the
Word of God, what the Bible says about being a
believer in Christ Jesus as it relates to wealth, riches,
blessings, abundance, and prosperity.

First all of let's make it perfectly clear that although
we will have the poor with us always, it is not God's
will that his children lack, live in poverty and be in
financial debt for the rest of our lives. God wants us
to live holy, have life more abundantly and live debt
free lives by faith.

Now many of us have had hard times financially and
we know that it does not mean that God is against us.
It may just mean that we need wisdom and to make
adjustments. God's Word teaches us patiently the
value of money, contentment and to trust in him for
every need. Phil 4:19 says, "And my God shall supply
all your need according to His riches in glory by
Christ Jesus."

The prerequisite to claim any of the promises of God
is to be a born believer in Christ Jesus, who has
accepted Jesus Christ as Lord and Savior.

The Bible says in Proverbs 28:13, "He who covers his sins will not prosper, but whoever confesses and forsakes them will have mercy."

We do know that there are many unsaved people who are prospering in a physical sense, yet they are not prospering in a spiritual sense!

It is confirmed in 3 John 1:2, "Beloved, I pray that you may prosper in all things and be in health, just as your soul prospers."

So to the extent that your soul prospers, God desires that you would prosper and be in good health as well. So in order for us to truly prosper spiritually, physically, mentally and financially, we must repent of our sins and accept Jesus Christ as LORD and Savior. Make no mistake; you can still prosper in the world without Christ! BUT it is a worldly temporary prosperity! Just as God can prosper you, the devil will also prosper you on his terms!

As a matter of fact, the Bible says the following:

Mark 8:35-37 KJV
35 For whosoever will save his life shall lose it; but whosoever shall lose his life for my sake and the gospel's, the same shall save it.
36 For what shall it profit a man, if he shall gain the whole world, and lose his own soul?
37 Or what shall a man give in exchange for his soul?

According to scripture we can prosper God's way, or the world's way! Remember the devil told Jesus that he could give him whatever he wanted if he bowed down and worshipped him! This is an interesting statement because many people have been deceived into worshipping the devil for fame and fortune, but Jesus did not entertain the devils offer! Let's read!

Luke 4:5-7 NKJV
5 Then the devil, taking Him up on a high mountain, showed Him all the kingdoms of the world in a moment of time.
6 And the devil said to Him, "All this authority I will give you, and their glory; for this has been delivered to me, and I give it to whomever I wish.
7 therefore, if you will worship before me, all will be yours."

So the devil can also prosper you but he wants you to worship him. Our only response is the response of Jesus Christ:

"And Jesus answered and said unto him, Get thee behind me, Satan: for it is written, Thou shalt worship the Lord thy God, and him only shalt thou serve." Luke 4:8 KJV

 Remember what Jesus said in John 10:10,

"The thief does not come except to steal, and to kill, and to destroy. I have come that they may have life, and that they may have it more abundantly."
John 10:10 NKJV

Two things to remember about God's prosperity and the devils prosperity. God gives freedom and the devil puts you in bondage. Jesus will always give us freedom but the devil's prosperity comes with a price! It is so much better to have God's prosperity through salvation in Christ because he owns it all anyway! Listen to what King David said:

Psalms 24:1-5 NKJV
1 A Psalm of David. The earth is the LORD's, and all its fullness, the world and those who dwell therein.
2 For He has founded it upon the seas, and established it upon the waters.
3 Who may ascend into the hill of the LORD? Or who may stand in His holy place?
4 He who has clean hands and a pure heart, who has not lifted up his soul to an idol, nor sworn deceitfully.
5 He shall receive blessing from the LORD, and righteousness from the God of his salvation.

Our Father in Heaven owns everything in the earth and he will bless, favor and prosper whomsoever he desires! Why? Because created it! Listen to what the Psalmist said:

Psalms 50:10-12 KJV
10 For every beast of the forest is mine, and the cattle upon a thousand hills.
11 I know all the fowls of the mountains: and the wild beasts of the field are mine.
12 If I were hungry, I would not tell thee: for the world is mine, and the fullness thereof.

Psa 89:11 confirms it! "The heavens are yours, the earth also is yours; the world and all its fullness, you have founded them."

The Bible also says in Prov 10:22 "The blessing of the LORD makes one rich, And He adds no sorrow with it."

When we speak about prosperity, there are a couple of things I want to make clear. I do not consider myself a prosperity preacher. I am a preacher and teacher of the Gospel of the Kingdom, and our LORD Jesus Christ, who teaches the whole council of God. My desire is to see God's people come to the full realization of who they are in Christ.

And because you are a child of God, you are entitled to walk victoriously, blessed of the Lord, living a joyful, prosperous life, free from the indulgences of the world. But there is one prerequisite; we must stay in faith, stay prayed up, be led by the spirit, and standing on the promises of God. The LORD will do his part, when we stand strong in the Word of God, because he is not a man that he should lie. Let's read!

Psalms 25:12-14 NKJV
12 Who is the man that fears the LORD? Him shall He teach in the way He chooses.
13 He himself shall dwell in prosperity, and his descendants shall inherit the earth.
14 The secret of the LORD is with those who fear Him; and He will show them His covenant.

As a child of God, the promises of God belong to you! Remember what Paul told us in Gal 3:26-29.

Galatians 3:26-29 KJV
26 For ye are all the children of God by faith in Christ Jesus.
27 For as many of you as have been baptized into Christ have put on Christ.

28 There is neither Jew nor Greek, there is neither bond nor free, there is neither male nor female: for ye are all one in Christ Jesus.
29 And if ye be Christ's, then are ye Abraham's seed, and heirs according to the promise.
Paul confirms it in other scriptures as well.

Ephesians 3:6 NKJV
6 that the Gentiles should be fellow heirs of the same body, and partakers of His promise in Christ through the gospel.

Romans 8:16-18 NKJV
16 The Spirit Himself bears witness with our spirit that we are children of God,
17 and if children, then heirs—heirs of God and joint heirs with Christ, if indeed we suffer with Him, that we may also be glorified together.
18 For I consider that the sufferings of this present time are not worthy to be compared with the glory which shall be revealed in us.

We cannot talk about prosperity and blessings without talking about giving. There have been a lot of things taught in the church about giving, sowing and reaping, but more importantly we must understand that God searches the heart of the giver. Let's read what Jesus said!

Mark 12:41-44 NKJV
41 Now Jesus sat opposite the treasury and saw how the people put money into the treasury, and many who were rich put in much.
42 Then one poor widow came and threw in two mites, which make a quadrans.

43 So He called His disciples to Himself and said to them, "Assuredly, I say to you that this poor widow has put in more than all those who have given to the treasury;
44 for they all put in out of their abundance, but she out of her poverty put in all that she had, her whole livelihood."

Jesus said that the widow gave all that she had basically from her heart. Others gave out of their abundance, but what moved Jesus was that this woman gave all she had, although it was a small amount.

Giving is a part of the Gospel. It is also our Christian duty. I don't believe that a person can truly fulfill their purpose without a sacrificial heart that gives. Why Because God is the greatest giver that ever existed and because we have his spirit, we also give!

Giving our best offering to the LORD brings blessing as well. The first time we see this is between Cain and Abel, where they both brought an offering to the LORD.

Genesis 4:3-5 NKJV
3 And in the process of time it came to pass that Cain brought an offering of the fruit of the ground to the LORD.
4 Abel also brought of the firstborn of his flock and of their fat. And the LORD respected Abel and his offering,
5 but He did not respect Cain and his offering. And Cain was very angry, and his countenance fell.

Heb 11:14 confirms that Abel offered a better sacrifice than Cain because he gave of the firstborn of his flock which was a pure lamb. Cain gave a gift that came from the ground, in which the ground was cursed according to Gen 3:17. I'm sure that Cain gave what he thought God would accept, but God rejected it and told him to do better. (Gen 4:6-7)

How many of us know that when we give something to God, it should be the very best that we have. We cannot give God scraps and cursed things! I find it absolutely amazing that people find it hard to give to give back to God what belongs to him. He is God and he deserves our very best! Abel's sacrifice emulated that which the Father would do with his Son Jesus Christ thousands of years later! Did not he give us his best? So why would we give God less if he deserves our best! The book of Hebrews says that Abel's offering was so pleasing, that we are still testifying about it today!

Hebrews 11:4 NKJV
4 By faith Abel offered to God a more excellent sacrifice than Cain, through which he obtained witness that he was righteous, God testifying of his gifts; and through it he being dead still speaks.

We have to understand that giving is very important in the Kingdom of God. When we give, which is sowing, we will reap back what we have sown! There are many scriptures that confirm this!

Proverbs 3:9-10 NKJV
9 Honor the LORD with your possessions, and with the first fruits of all your increase;
10 So your barns will be filled with plenty, and your

vats will overflow with new wine.

Proverbs 11:24-26 NKJV
24 There is one who scatters, yet increases more; and there is one who withholds more than is right, But it leads to poverty.
25 The generous soul will be made rich, and he who waters will also be watered himself.
26 The people will curse him who withholds grain, but blessing will be on the head of him who sells it.

Proverbs 11:28 NKJV
28 He who trusts in his riches will fall, but the righteous will flourish like foliage.

Proverbs 22:4 NKJV
4 By humility and the fear of the LORD Are riches and honor and life.

Proverbs 22:9 NKJV
9 He who has a generous eye will be blessed, for he gives of his bread to the poor.

Luke 6:38 NKJV
38 Give and it will be given to you: good measure, pressed down, shaken together, and running over will be put into your bosom. For with the same measure that you use, it will be measured back to you."

2 Corinthians 9:5-8 NKJV
5 Therefore I thought it necessary to exhort the brethren to go to you ahead of time, and prepare your generous gift beforehand, which you had previously promised, that it may be ready as a matter of generosity and not as a grudging obligation.
6 But this I say: He who sows sparingly will also reap

sparingly, and he who sows bountifully will also reap bountifully.

7 So let each one give as he purposes in his heart, not grudgingly or of necessity; for God loves a cheerful giver.

8 And God is able to make all grace abound toward you, that you, always having all sufficiency in all things, may have abundance for every good work.

Col 3:17 And whatever you do in word or deed, do all in the name of the Lord Jesus, giving thanks to God the Father through Him.

Col 3:23 And whatever you do, do it heartily, as to the Lord and not to men,

Col 3:24 knowing that from the Lord you will receive the reward of the inheritance; for you serve the Lord Christ.

As we can see, the Bible is full of scripture as it relates to giving. The Bible says that every word shall be established on the testimony of two or three witness in 1 Cor 13:1. When we are obedient to the Word of God, we will see the manifestation of all that God has promised in his Word. Why? Because God fulfills his covenant promises to his obedient children who stand strong in his Word!

The scriptures say in Pro 16:20:
"He who heeds the word wisely will find good, and whoever trusts in the LORD, happy is he."

The word "happy" means prosperous, blessed or harmonious.

Psalms 1:1-3 NKJV
1 Blessed is the man who walks not in the counsel of

the ungodly, nor stands in the path of sinners, nor sits in the seat of the scornful;

2 But his delight is in the law of the LORD, and in His law he meditates day and night.

3 He shall be like a tree planted by the rivers of water, that brings forth its fruit in its season, whose leaf also shall not wither; and whatever he does shall prosper.

When God blesses us and prospers us, we must stay humble and never forget where that wealth came from!

Deuteronomy 8:18 NKJV

18 "And you shall remember the LORD your God, for it is He who gives you power to get wealth, that He may establish His covenant which He swore to your fathers, as it is this day.

We must never forget that every good and perfect gift comes from God! We must always stay focused, humble, gracious, thankful and compassionate!

We must never allow prosperity to deceive us. Some people are led astray by money, and most of the time it involves POWER, MONEY, and SEX with money leading the charge. Look what the LORD Jesus and the Apostle Paul said about riches and money.

Matthew 6:19-24 NKJV

19 "Do not lay up for yourselves treasures on earth, where moth and rust destroy and where thieves break in and steal;

20 but lay up for yourselves treasures in heaven, where neither moth nor rust destroys and where thieves do not break in and steal.

21 For where your treasure is, there your heart will be

also.

1 Timothy 6:6-10 NKJV
6 Now godliness with contentment is great gain.
7 For we brought nothing into this world, and it is certain we can carry nothing out.
8 And having food and clothing, with these we shall be content.
9 But those who desire to be rich fall into temptation and a snare, and into many foolish and harmful lusts which drown men in destruction and perdition.
10 For the love of money is a root of all kinds of evil, for which some have strayed from the faith in their greediness, and pierced themselves through with many sorrows.

As it relates to our purpose sometimes the LORD will require that we sacrifice our riches for the sake of the Kingdom. There was a rich man who wanted to know how he could have eternal life. Jesus told him the following:

Matthew 19:21 NKJV
21 Jesus said to him, "If you want to be perfect, go, sell what you have and give to the poor, and you will have treasure in heaven; and come, follow me."

The man was so rich that it was impossible for him to give up his riches for the riches of the Kingdom of God!

Sometimes we can get comfortable in our riches and put them before God, but that is a big mistake as well! Jesus told a parable about a rich man who had a whole lot of stuff, and wanted more stuff, but he was not rich toward God!

Luke 12:15-21 NKJV

15 And He said to them, "Take heed and beware of covetousness, for one's life does not consist in the abundance of the things he possesses."

16 Then He spoke a parable to them, saying: "The ground of a certain rich man yielded plentifully.

17 And he thought within himself, saying, 'What shall I do, since I have no room to store my crops?'

18 So he said, 'I will do this: I will pull down my barns and build greater, and there I will store all my crops and my goods.

19 And I will say to my soul, "Soul, you have many goods laid up for many years; take your ease; eat, drink, and be merry." '

20 But God said to him, 'Fool! This night your soul will be required of you; then whose will those things be which you have provided?'

21"So is he who lays up treasure for himself, and is not rich toward God."

God is not against us having wealth and riches, just as long as it doesn't have you! God desires that we be found faithful in riches. When we have been found faithful in riches and wealth, God will then commit to our trust the true riches of the Kingdom of God!

Luke 16:10-13 NKJV

10 He who is faithful in what is least is faithful also in much; and he who is unjust in what is least is unjust also in much.

11 Therefore if you have not been faithful in the unrighteous mammon, who will commit to your trust the true riches?

12 And if you have not been faithful in what is another man's, who will give you what is your own?

13 No servant can serve two masters; for

either he will hate the one and love the other, or else he will be loyal to the one and despise the other. You cannot serve God and mammon.

The lesson of prosperity is this. One should never make a judgment regarding a person's spirituality based on his or her prosperity in the world. The LORD told the disciples that God makes His sun rise on both the evil and the good, and His rain to fall on both the just and the unjust.

Mat 5:44 But I say to you, love your enemies, bless those who curse you, do good to those who hate you, and pray for those who spitefully use you and persecute you,
Mat 5:45 that you may be sons of your Father in heaven; for He makes His sun rise on the evil and on the good, and sends rain on the just and on the unjust.

So as we see, God desires to bless his people abundantly, but we must have a balance. So the question is, "What should be our attitude toward prosperity and riches?" As children of God we have been given precious promises from God concerning prosperity in his Word. Yet, we should be humble, gracious, and content with a giving heart toward God and others!

Protection

"No weapon formed against you shall prosper, and every tongue which rises against you in judgment you shall condemn. This is the heritage of the servants of the LORD, and their righteousness is from me, Says the LORD."
Isaiah 54:17 NKJV

One of the most profound promises of God is divine protection. The LORD has always protected his beloved righteous children. There are so many scriptures and examples in the Bible that speak to us about the protection of God. In the first book of the Bible; Genesis, God protected Noah and his family in the ark from the judgment of the flood.

Genesis 7:1 NKJV
1 Then the LORD said to Noah, "Come into the ark, you and all your household, because I have seen that you are righteous before me in this generation.

Notice that God recognized Noah's righteousness, in the midst of all the unrighteousness!

When God spoke to Abraham to leave his Father's house and country, he gave him the promise of protection!

Genesis 12:1-3 NKJV
1 Now the LORD had said to Abram: "Get out of your country, from your family and from your father's house, to a land that I will show you.
2 I will make you a great nation; I will bless you and make your name great; and you shall be a blessing.

3 I will bless those who bless you, and I will curse him who curses you; and in you all the families of the earth shall be blessed."

God also protected Lot and his family from the judgment that was sent upon Sodom and Gomorrah.

Genesis 19:12-13 NKJV
12 Then the men said to Lot, "Have you anyone else here? Son-in-law, your sons, your daughters, and whomever you have in the city—take them out of this place!
13 For we will destroy this place, because the outcry against them has grown great before the face of the LORD, and the LORD has sent us to destroy it."

All throughout the Bible there is the promise of protection for the people of God as we abide and take refuge in him.   All throughout the Bible we find God protecting his people from the hand of the enemy, famine, pestilence and the sword. The children of Israel knew that God has promised them protection but they had to abide in him and in his Word.

Pro 18:10 says, "The name of the LORD is a strong tower; the righteous run to it and are safe."

When we think about that scripture, it says that the name of the LORD is a strong tower, a refuge, and place of complete safety to all that trust in him and abide in him. Maybe this is why David wrote wonderful Psalms about the LORD. Let's take a look at a few of them.

Psalms 23:4 KJV
4 Yea, though I walk through the valley of the shadow

of death, I will fear no evil: for thou art with me; thy rod and thy staff they comfort me.

David said that when he walks through the valley of the shadow of death, he would fear no evil. Why? Because the LORD is with him, and his rod and staff comfort him.

David also said in Psalm 27:1; The LORD is my light and my salvation; whom shall I fear? The LORD is the strength of my life; of whom shall I be afraid?

David who was delivered from Goliath the giant said, "The LORD is my light and salvation, whom shall I fear, the LORD is the strength of my life, of whom shall I be afraid." In verse 2, he expounds even further by saying:

Psa 27:2 when the wicked came against me to eat up my flesh, my enemies and foes, they stumbled and fell.
Psa 27:3 though an army may encamp against me, my heart shall not fear; though war may rise against me, in this I will be confident.
Psa 27:4 one thing I have desired of the LORD, that will I seek after: That I may dwell in the house of the LORD All the days of my life, to behold the beauty of the LORD, And to inquire in His temple.
Psa 27:5 for in the time of trouble He shall hide me in His pavilion; in the secret place of His tabernacle He shall hide me; He shall set me high upon a rock.

David recognized that his help and protection were from the LORD and that no matter what came against him he was confident that God would protect him and cover him. Again he writes in Psalm 91:

Psalms 91:1-6 NKJV
1 He who dwells in the secret place of the Most High
Shall abide under the shadow of the Almighty.
2 I will say of the LORD, "He is my refuge and my
fortress; My God, in Him I will trust."
3 Surely He shall deliver you from the snare of the
fowler and from the perilous pestilence.
4 He shall cover you with His feathers, and under His
wings you shall take refuge; His truth shall be your
shield and buckler.
5 You shall not be afraid of the terror by night, nor of
the arrow that flies by day,
6 Nor of the pestilence that walks in darkness, nor of
the destruction that lays waste at noonday.

When we read these passages of scripture we see that
David understood that if he abided in the LORD that
God would cover him and protect him.

In the last few passages of Psalm 91, David shares
this and mentions salvation in which we are covered
by the blood of Jesus, which is very important for us
as New Testament believers in Christ.

Psalms 91:14-16 KJV
14 Because he hath set his love upon me, therefore
will I deliver him: I will set him on high, because he
has known my name.
15 He shall call upon me, and I will answer him: I will
be with him in trouble; I will deliver him, and honor
him.
16 With long life will I satisfy him, and shew him my
salvation.

Child of God did you hear that? The LORD said through his servant David, "Because he has set his love upon me, I will deliver him, and I will set him on high because he has known my name." He then says, "He shall call upon me, and I will answer him, I will be with him in trouble. I will deliver him and honor him, and with long life I will satisfy him, and show him my salvation!

Do you see the divine protection of God in this passage of scripture? God said I will deliver him, I will be with him in trouble, and I will show him my salvation!

The word salvation in the Hebrew is "yesh-oo'-aw" or Yeshua which means something saved, deliverance, aid, victory, prosperity, health, help, salvation, saving health, and welfare. *(Strong's Talking Greek & Hebrew Dictionary.)*

So prophetically David is giving us a glimpse of the one who would provide salvation for every one that believes on his name, and that name is Jesus!

Remember we said that according to Proverbs 18:10, "The name of the LORD is a strong tower; the righteous run to it and are safe."

The LORD Jesus death at the cross provided salvation for every believer. Which means that we have deliverance, aid, victory, health, and help! Remember the scripture says that the promises of God are yes and amen! God made a covenant promise to Abraham that he would bless them that blessed him, and curse them that cursed him. (Gen 12:3)

We also find throughout the Bible that because of these covenant promises that the children of Israel were blessed by God with divine protection as long as they abided by the covenant promises through their obedience. When God made a covenant the children of Israel, the primary conditions were faith and obedience!

Time after time in the Bible we find that God protected his people. When the Children of Israel took possession of the Promised Land under the leadership of Joshua, they conquered many enemies and God gave them victory. Out of all of the battles that Joshua and the Children of Israel fought, he lost only one battle, and that was the "Battle of Ai."

Listen to what the LORD said to Joshua:

Joshua 7:6-7 NKJV
6 Then Joshua tore his clothes, and fell to the earth on his face before the ark of the LORD until evening, he and the elders of Israel; and they put dust on their heads.
7 And Joshua said, "Alas, Lord GOD, why have You brought this people over the Jordan at all—to deliver us into the hand of the Amorites, to destroy us? Oh, that we had been content, and dwelt on the other side of the Jordan!

And the LORD responded:

Joshua 7:10-11 NKJV
10 So the LORD said to Joshua: "Get up! Why do you lie thus on your face?
11 Israel has sinned, and they have also transgressed my covenant which I commanded them. For they

have even taken some of the accursed things, and have both stolen and deceived; and they have also put it among their own stuff.

The reason why Joshua lost the battle is because of disobedience in the camp. After the Battle of Jericho, God instructed them not to take anything from that battle because it was cursed. Everything was to go to the LORD, but Achan who was among the Israelites stole a beautiful robe, and silver and gold, thus bringing judgment from the LORD.

Joshua 7:20-21 NKJV
20 And Achan answered Joshua and said, "Indeed I have sinned against the LORD God of Israel, and this is what I have done:
21 When I saw among the spoils a beautiful Babylonian garment, two hundred shekels of silver, and a wedge of gold weighing fifty shekels, I coveted them and took them. And there they are, hidden in the earth in the midst of my tent, with the silver under it."

So the divine protection upon them was lifted because someone disobeyed the commandment of the LORD!

Joshua 7:25 NKJV
25 And Joshua said, "Why have you troubled us? The LORD will trouble you this day." So all Israel stoned him with stones; and they burned them with fire after they had stoned them with stones.

Right after Israel set its house in order, God gave them victory over the people of "Ai." Let's read!
Joshua 8:1-2 NKJV

1 Now the LORD said to Joshua: "Do not be afraid, nor be dismayed; take all the people of war with you, and arise, go up to Ai. See, I have given into your hand the king of Ai, his people, his city, and his land. 2 And you shall do to Ai and its king as you did to Jericho and its king. Only its spoil and its cattle you shall take as booty for yourselves. Lay an ambush for the city behind it."

Joshua 8:25-28 NKJV
25 So it was that all who fell that day, both men and women, were twelve thousand—all the people of Ai.
26 For Joshua did not draw back his hand, with which he stretched out the spear, until he had utterly destroyed all the inhabitants of Ai.
27 Only the livestock and the spoil of that city Israel took as booty for themselves, according to the word of the LORD which He had commanded Joshua.
28 So Joshua burned Ai and made it a heap forever, a desolation to this day.

When God gives us his promises, the prerequisite is faith and obedience to his Word. God will always keep his Word, but we must trust God through our faith and obedience to receive the divine protection that he has promised us in his Word.

One of the most profound victories in scripture is the victory that God gave Jehoshaphat in 2 Chronicles 20. We know from the Bible that Jehoshaphat was a godly king and did right in the sight of the LORD, because he walked in the ways of his father David.

Let's read the account in 2 Chronicles 17:3-5 NKJV

3 Now the LORD was with Jehoshaphat, because he walked in the former ways of his father David; he did not seek the Baals,
4 but sought the God of his father, and walked in His commandments and not according to the acts of Israel.
5 Therefore the LORD established the kingdom in his hand; and all Judah gave presents to Jehoshaphat, and he had riches and honor in abundance.

So we see from the start that he obeyed the LORD following in the ways of King David, therefore God granted him prosperity and divine protection. As a matter of fact in 2 Chronicles chapter 20, when three enemies came against Judah, he cried out to the LORD in prayer and fasting and God gave them victory.

2 Chronicles 20:1-4 NKJV
1 It happened after this that the people of Moab with the people of Ammon, and others with them besides the Ammonites, came to battle against Jehoshaphat.
2 Then some came and told Jehoshaphat, saying, "A great multitude is coming against you from beyond the sea, from Syria; and they are in Hazazon Tamar" (which is En Gedi).
3 And Jehoshaphat feared, and set himself to seek the LORD, and proclaimed a fast throughout all Judah.
4 So Judah gathered together to ask help from the LORD; and from all the cities of Judah they came to seek the LORD.

To get the full understanding of the story you can read the entire account in 2 Chronicles 20 verses 1-32. You can also read about it in my book: *The Power of Prayer, Prophecy and Praise* in which I expound and exposit the entire account of the story with commentary.

After Jehoshaphat and the people of Judah prayed and fasted, he called on the name of the LORD, and invoked the covenant promises made to father Abraham, who was called the friend of God. (James 2:23)

2 Chronicles 20:5-9 NKJV
5 Then Jehoshaphat stood in the assembly of Judah and Jerusalem, in the house of the LORD, before the new court,
6 and said: "O LORD God of our fathers, are You not God in heaven, and do You not rule over all the kingdoms of the nations, and in Your hand is there not power and might, so that no one is able to withstand You?
7 Are you not our God, who drove out the inhabitants of this land before your people Israel, and gave it to the descendants of Abraham Your friend forever?
8 And they dwell in it, and have built you a sanctuary in it for your name, saying,
9 'If disaster comes upon us—sword, judgment, pestilence, or famine—we will stand before this temple and in your presence (for your name is in this temple), and cry out to you in our affliction, and You will hear and save.'

So King Jehoshaphat called on the name of the LORD and invoked the name of Abraham in whom God made the covenant promises to the children of Israel! Listen to Jehoshaphat as cries out to the LORD in prayer and asks God for divine protection!

2 Chronicles 20:12 NKJV
12 O our God, will you not judge them? For we have no power against this great multitude that is coming against us; nor do we know what to do, but our eyes are upon You."

After they prayed and cried out to the LORD, the LORD gave them a Word through the Prophet Jahaziel (2 Chron 20:14) and said:

2 Chronicles 20:17 NKJV
17 You will not need to fight in this battle. Position yourselves, stand still and see the salvation of the LORD, who is with you, O Judah and Jerusalem!' Do not fear or be dismayed; tomorrow go out against them, for the LORD is with you."

The end of the story is profound! God hears the humble prayer and cry of Jehoshaphat. He gives them a prophetic word, to go out against the enemy with praise and he would give them a great deliverance!

It all started with the covenant promise of protection that God has given to all of his beloved children, and it was manifested through prayer, prophecy and praise! Hallelujah!

2 Chronicles 20:21-23 NKJV
21 And when he had consulted with the people, he appointed those who should sing to the LORD, and who should praise the beauty of holiness, as they went out before the army and were saying: "Praise the LORD, For His mercy endures forever."
22 Now when they began to sing and to praise, the LORD set ambushes against the people of Ammon,

Moab, and Mount Seir, who had come against Judah; and they were defeated.

23 For the people of Ammon and Moab stood up against the inhabitants of Mount Seir to utterly kill and destroy them. And when they had made an end of the inhabitants of Seir, they helped to destroy one another.

People of God, do you not see that we are covered and protected by the LORD. It doesn't matter whether it is famine, pestilence, or the sword. God will always protect his beloved children who walk in righteousness, holiness, and the truth of his Word!

Even in the Passover story of Exodus 12, God gives us a glimpse of the divine protection by the blood of the Lamb Jesus Christ. As the LORD was about to deliver them from the bondage of Egypt, and to strike the firstborn of Egypt. God gave them instructions to take of a lamb of the first year, without spot, blemish or defect and to slay it. They were instructed to put the blood on the top and sides of the doorpost of their homes, and the destroyer would pass them by!

Exodus 12:5-7 NKJV
5 Your lamb shall be without blemish, a male of the first year. You may take it from the sheep or from the goats.
6 Now you shall keep it until the fourteenth day of the same month. Then the whole assembly of the congregation of Israel shall kill it at twilight.
7 And they shall take some of the blood and put it on the two doorposts and on the lintel of the houses where they eat it.

Exodus 12:12-13 NKJV

12 'For I will pass through the land of Egypt on that night, and will strike all the firstborn in the land of Egypt, both man and beast; and against all the gods of Egypt I will execute judgment: I am the LORD. 13 Now the blood shall be a sign for you on the houses where you are. And when I see the blood, I will pass over you; and the plague shall not be on you to destroy you when I strike the land of Egypt.

People of God this is so profound. Because we know that Jesus was that Passover Lamb of God whose blood was put on the doorposts of the Israelites homes. The revelation is that Jesus is the Lamb of God that took away the sins of the world. He covered us and took all of our sins at the cross of Calvary with his blood!

The Apostle Paul said:

Colossians 1:13-14 NKJV
13 He has delivered us from the power of darkness and conveyed us into the kingdom of the Son of His love,
14 in whom we have redemption through His blood, the forgiveness of sins.

We are covered by the blood with divine protection! You should take this opportunity to praise and give God glory for his divine promise of protection that he has given to you and your family, and all that believe!

Provision

"And give my son Solomon a loyal heart to keep your commandments and your testimonies and your statutes, to do all these things, and to build the temple for which I have made provision."
1 Chronicles 29:19 NKJV

King David was known as a man after God's heart, and his desire was to build a temple for the LORD God. Yet God told him that he would not be able to do it, but his son would do it. Despite not being able to lead the building of the Temple, David made provision for Solomon to start the project!

1 Chronicles 28:2-3 NKJV
2 Then King David rose to his feet and said, "Hear me, my brethren and my people: I had it in my heart to build a house of rest for the ark of the covenant of the LORD, and for the footstool of our God, and had made preparations to build it.
3 But God said to me, 'You shall not build a house for My name, because you have been a man of war and have shed blood.'

1 Chronicles 28:6 NKJV
6 Now He said to me, 'It is your son Solomon who shall build my house and my courts; for I have chosen him to be My son, and I will be his Father.

So the LORD told David that he would not be able to build the temple but grace would be given to his son Solomon to build it. As a result, David provided everything that Solomon would need to start the building of the Temple. In other words, there was provision for the building of the temple.

What does provision mean? Provision is the action of providing or supplying something for use. It is an amount or thing supplied or provided.

Listen to the provisions that David made for the temple building project.

1 Chronicles 28:11-15 NKJV
11 Then David gave his son Solomon the plans for the vestibule, its houses, its treasuries, its upper chambers, its inner chambers, and the place of the mercy seat;
12 and the plans for all that he had by the Spirit, of the courts of the house of the LORD, of all the chambers all around, of the treasuries of the house of God, and of the treasuries for the dedicated things;
13 also for the division of the priests and the Levites, for all the work of the service of the house of the LORD, and for all the articles of service in the house of the LORD.
14 He gave gold by weight for things of gold, for all articles used in every kind of service; also silver for all articles of silver by weight, for all articles used in every kind of service;
15 the weight for the lampstands of gold, and their lamps of gold, by weight for each lampstand and its lamps; for the lampstands of silver by weight, for the lampstand and its lamps, according to the use of each lampstand.

Isn't this an amazing story? Although David did not start or complete the work, he made provision for his son to succeed in building the house of the LORD.

He gave him the plans and provided large amounts of gold and silver for the building project. The revelation in this promise of provision is if a human father gave his son what he needed to succeed; will not our Heavenly Father who is even greater than a human father give us the provision to succeed?

When God gives you purpose he supplies you with provision and everything you need to succeed. He gives you divine direction; He gives you people, He gives you favor, he gives you wisdom, knowledge and understanding. He gives you talents, abilities creativity, and above all the Holy Spirit, who will lead you and guide you into all truth!

When we look at examples in scripture, God always provided for his people! He took care of the Israelites in the wilderness. The Bible says that he gave them manna from heaven, and their shoes and their clothes did not wear out!

Nehemiah 9:20-21 NKJV
20 You also gave your good Spirit to instruct them, and did not withhold your manna from their mouth, and gave them water for their thirst.
21 Forty years you sustained them in the wilderness; they lacked nothing; their clothes did not wear out and their feet did not swell.

In other words God supplied all of their needs with divine provisions from heaven. David understood the great mercies of God as well and said in Psalm 37:

Psalms 37:25 NKJV
25 I have been young, and now am old; yet I have not seen the righteous forsaken, nor his descendants

begging bread.

Why would David say this? Because God will supply all of our need according to his riches in glory! Paul mentions this in Philippians 4 verses 10-20 concerning the Philippian church. Paul in his missionary journeys trusted God to meet every need as he preached and shared the Gospel. The Philippian church was a great blessing to Paul. He stated that no other churches shared with him concerning giving and receiving, they were the only one.

Philippians 4:15-20 NKJV
15 Now you Philippians know also that in the beginning of the gospel, when I departed from Macedonia, no church shared with me concerning giving and receiving but you only.
16 For even in Thessalonica you sent aid once and again for my necessities.
17 Not that I seek the gift, but I seek the fruit that abounds to your account.
18 Indeed I have all and abound. I am full, having received from Epaphroditus the things sent from you, a sweet-smelling aroma, an acceptable sacrifice, well pleasing to God.
19 And my God shall supply all your need according to His riches in glory by Christ Jesus.
20 Now to our God and Father be glory forever and ever. Amen.

Paul then praises them for their kindness and compassion in supplying the needs of the Man of God while he ministered the Word of God. This is powerful, because Paul is praising them for the divine provisions from God in taking care of him! As a result, Paul tells them, "Because you met my need, God will supply or make provision for all of your need! Isn't this wonderful? Paul in his missionary journeys labored as a tent maker to make a living, (Acts 18:3) but I am sure at times it got tough, and he mentions the church at Philippi that gave him an offering. How many of us know that what we make happen for others, God will make happen for us also? God will use anything or anyone to supernaturally supply our needs.

In the book of Kings Chapter 17, many of us know the story of Elijah who prophesied by the Word of the LORD that there would be no rain in Israel because of the sin of Ahab who was married to Jezebel. During the drought and famine, God used a raven to feed Elijah and he drank water from the Brook Cherith. Here we see the divine provision of God as it relates to God's divine purpose for our lives.

1 Kings 17:2-7 NKJV
2 Then the word of the LORD came to him, saying,
3 "Get away from here and turn eastward, and hide by the Brook Cherith, which flows into the Jordan.
4 And it will be that you shall drink from the brook, and I have commanded the ravens to feed you there."
5 So he went and did according to the word of the LORD, for he went and stayed by the Brook Cherith, which flows into the Jordan.
6 The ravens brought him bread and meat in the morning, and bread and meat in the evening; and he drank from the brook.
7 And it happened after a while that the brook dried up, because there had been no rain in the land.

It is amazing that God used Ravens to feed the

Prophet of God. Ravens by nature are scavengers and predators. They don't share their good, they hunt for food, but God supernaturally commanded a Raven (bird) to bring him food and provide for the Prophet!

After the Brook dried up, God commanded Elijah to go to Zaraphath where provision would be made again for him by a widow.

1 Kings 17:8-9 NKJV
8 Then the word of the LORD came to him, saying,
9 "Arise, go to Zarephath, which belongs to Sidon, and dwell there. See, I have commanded a widow there to provide for you."

Then in 1 Kings 19, the provision of God is made again as Elijah runs for his life from Jezebel. This time God uses an angel to provide for the Man of God.

1 Kings 19:5-7 NKJV
5 Then as he lay and slept under a broom tree, suddenly an angel touched him, and said to him, "Arise and eat."
6 Then he looked, and there by his head was a cake baked on coals, and a jar of water. So he ate and drank, and lay down again.
7 And the angel of the LORD came back the second time, and touched him, and said, "Arise and eat, because the journey is too great for you."

Isn't this amazing? We see that God can use a bird, a human being or an angel to supernaturally provide for those whom he has called according to his purpose. When we think back over our lives, we can see how God made a way out of no way, and has always supplied our need! As a Pastor, I have seen God do miraculous things in our ministry!

I am reminded of a song that says: *"God will make a way, when there seems to be no way. He works in ways we cannot see. He will make a way for me. He will be my guide, hold me closely to his side. With love and strength for each new day, he will make a way, God will make a way!"*

God has truly made a way out of no way over the years and has blessed our church, the people of God and my family with provision and blessings from heaven! I have heard so many testimonies of God's great grace where he has blessed his people. Child of God, always remember that supernatural provision is available for you as you fulfill the divine purpose of God!

CHAPTER 6

PROPHECY

"So shall my word be that goes forth from my mouth;
It shall not return to me void, But it shall accomplish
what I please, and it shall prosper in the thing for
which I sent it."
Isaiah 55:11 NKJV

When we think about prophecy, the question that should come to our mind is what God has predestined, purposed, planned, and promised in his Word concerning my life. There are so many scriptures where God is speaking, decreeing and declaring his Word to the children of Israel so that they understood that God had a wonderful plan for their lives.

The most profound thing about God's Word is that what God has spoken will surely come to pass. Numbers 23:19 says something profound:

Numbers 23:19 NKJV
19 God is not a man, that He should lie, nor a son of man, that He should repent. Has He said, and will He not do? Or has He spoken, and will He not make it good?

This powerful word was spoken by Balaam the Son of Beor, a non-Israelite who was a Prophet. He was hired to curse Israel by Balak the King, but since God had blessed his people, he could not curse them. You can read about Balaam in Numbers chapter 22-25.

How many of us know that what God has blessed, no man can curse! Remember the covenant promise to Abraham in Gen 12:1-3 KJV

1 Now the LORD had said to Abram: "Get out of your country, from your family and from your father's house, to a land that I will show you.
2 I will make you a great nation; I will bless you and make your name great; and you shall be a blessing.
3 I will bless those who bless you, and I will curse him who curses you; and in you all the families of the earth shall be blessed."

When God has a divine purpose for your life and orders your steps, there is no devil in hell or human being on earth who can stop it. Maybe this is why the Apostle Paul said in Romans 8:28-31 NKJV:

28 And we know that all things work together for good to those who love God, to those who are the called according to His purpose.
29 For whom He foreknew, He also predestined to be conformed to the image of His Son, that He might be the firstborn among many brethren.
30 Moreover whom He predestined, these He also called; whom He called, these He also justified; and whom He justified, these He also glorified.
31 What then shall we say to these things? If God is for us, who can be against us?

Did you hear what Paul said? All things are working together for your good. Why? Because you love him, and you have been called according to his purpose. He goes on to say if God predestined you, and justified you, he will also glorify you. He then says the profound thing in verse 31.

If God be for us, who can be against us? When you break this down, Paul is literally saying God has purposed and predestined you in the earth, and because he has done this, you are justified in his sight, and you will also be glorified with him. Not only that, but because he has done these things, who can stand against us? This is powerful. We need to understand that God's perfect will is going to be done in the earth, and all things are working together for your good and God's glory!

This is why we can never hate on anyone or what they are achieving and accomplishing for the Kingdom of God. Listen what Paul said:

Romans 14:4 NKJV
4 Who are you to judge another's servant? To his own master he stands or falls. Indeed, he will be made to stand, for God is able to make him stand.

Sometimes in the body of Christ, there are people who are so judgmental about other people who are laboring for Christ. One thing I have learned is to mind my own business, because I have my own purpose to accomplish for God! Many of us may remember when Peter was being nosy about the disciple John. Listen what Jesus said:

John 21:20-23 NKJV
20 Then Peter, turning around, saw the disciple whom Jesus loved following, who also had leaned on His breast at the supper, and said, "Lord, who is the one who betrays you?"
21 Peter, seeing him, said to Jesus, "But Lord, what about this man?"
22 Jesus said to him, "If I will that he remain till I

come, what is that to you? You follow me."
23 Then this saying went out among the brethren that this disciple would not die. Yet Jesus did not say to him that he would not die, but, "If I will that he remain till I come, what is that to you?

Peter was concerned about John's purpose and Jesus basically told Peter to mind his business. Look at the statement again in verse 22.

22 Jesus said to him, "If I will that he remain till I come, what is that to you? You follow me."

He then reiterates it again in verse 23.
"Then this saying went out among the brethren that this disciple would not die. Yet Jesus did not say to him that he would not die, but, "If I will that he remain till I come, what is that to you?"

This should speak volumes to each and every person under the sound of my voice. We all have a purpose to fulfill for the LORD. We should fight the good fight of faith, we should content for the faith, but mind our own business as it relates to our purpose in Christ.

Why? Because God is the one who causes us to stand or fall! Only the Most High God can cause or allow a man to stand or fall, so we should stop hating and pointing the finger at others who are not against us, but for us!

Now let's get back to Balaam and Balak!

When we look at verse 20 we find an interesting statement. Balaam says the following:

Numbers 23:20 NKJV
20 Behold, I have received a command to bless; He has blessed, and I cannot reverse it.

In other words God predestined, purposed, planned and promised many things concerning the children of Israel and nothing could undo it. Isaiah said the following concerning the LORD:

"So shall my word be that goes forth from my mouth; It shall not return to me void, But it shall accomplish what I please, and it shall prosper in the thing for which I sent it."
Isaiah 55:11 NKJV

God's prophetic Word is powerful and true and we see it all throughout the Bible concerning Israel, concerning the nations, and concerning his return. Even now as we see the things that are transpiring in the world today, we see God's Word coming to pass.

Isaiah said by the spirit of the LORD, "So shall my word be that goes forth out of my mouth. It will not return to be void." This means that what God has spoken will come to pass, and accomplish what he desires, and it will prosper in the thing for which he sent it.

There is another scripture that confirms what God has spoken will come to pass.

Isaiah 46:9-11 KJV
9 Remember the former things of old: for I am God, and there is none else; I am God, and there is none like me,
10 Declaring the end from the beginning, and from

ancient times the things that are not yet done, saying, my counsel shall stand, and I will do all my pleasure: 11 Calling a ravenous bird from the east, the man that executes my counsel from a far country: yea, I have spoken it, I will also bring it to pass; I have purposed it, I will also do it.

Isn't this a powerful scripture? God is literally saying that because I am God, I can do what I want to do according to my own sovereign will. He also said I have already predestined, purposed and planned it, and what I have spoken, I will do it! Why? Because my Word will not return unto me void according to Isaiah 55:11.

 One of the things we must understand about prophecy is that prophecy can be yesterday, today or tomorrow. Regardless of what the timeframe may be, God has spoken his Word through his servants the prophets and he watches over his Word to perform it.

Jeremiah 1:12 NKJV
12 Then the LORD said to me, "You have seen well, for I am ready to perform my word."

Many of you may have had someone prophesy over your life as it relates to your purpose in Christ. If it is of the LORD it will surely come to pass. In my book, *"The Power of Prayer, Prophecy and Praise,* I talk about prophetic words spoken over my life and the fulfillment of all that God has predestined, purposed, planned, and promised for my life.

As a child of God, you need to know that God has a plan for you, and that plan will not return unto him void. God told the Prophet Jeremiah that he knew him in his mother's womb.

Jeremiah 1:4-5 NKJV
4 Then the word of the LORD came to me, saying:
5 "Before I formed you in the womb I knew you;
before you were born I sanctified you; I ordained you
a prophet to the nations."

Isn't that amazing? God literally said, "Before your
mother and father even came together, I knew you
would be born. I want you to think about this
statement, because this is not just for Jeremiah the
Prophet. God knows you by name. Even through
there are billions of people in the earth, God knows
you by name.

He went on to tell Jeremiah, before you were even
born, I ordained you a prophet to the nations. God
said I knew you would be born and one day, it would
all come to pass! When I think about my own life,
and all that I went through, this brings me comfort
and it should bring you comfort.

The powerful thing is this: No matter what happens
in your life, whether it be sin, pain, hurt, trials,
tribulations, troubles or tragedies, God has a plan for
your life. When I look back over my life, and all that I
have been through, the good times, bad times,
painful times, tribulation times, and suffering times,
it was all for the glory of God.

All you have been through and where you are today,
has been because of decisions you made, and those
decisions have brought you to a place of purpose in
Christ Jesus our LORD!

CHAPTER 7

GOD'S DIVINE PURPOSE

When we think about many of the Saints in the Bible, and what they went through. God's divine purpose was manifested in their lives as the LORD prepared and positioned them for leading his people.

Many of them went through much pain and were persecuted, but God used that pain and persecution as an instrument of his righteousness to fulfill his divine purpose in the earth. The Bible is full of people who had a divine purpose for their life and they fulfilled it. This is a short list, but it is not the complete list! Many of us are familiar with them.

Moses, Joseph, David, Jabez, Daniel, Job, Paul, The Apostles and last but certainly not least, Jesus the Christ. Out of this entire list of names, the two that stand out are Joseph and the LORD Jesus Christ. Joseph is a type of Christ, or his life is a shadow of things to come concerning the LORD Jesus Christ.

Consider the life and story of Joseph. Joseph was the favorite of his father's eleven sons, and he had a dream that they would bow down to him. He was hated by his brothers; they called him a dreamer, spoke bad about him, stripped him of his nice jacket, and threw him in a pit. They then sold him to some slave traders for 20 pieces of silver, who then took him into Egypt, and sold him into slavery again.

Genesis 37:3-5 NKJV
3 Now Israel loved Joseph more than all his children,

because he was the son of his old age. Also he made him a tunic of many colors.

4 But when his brothers saw that their father loved him more than all his brothers, they hated him and could not speak peaceably to him.

5 Now Joseph had a dream, and he told it to his brothers; and they hated him even more.

His brothers were jealous because of the favor on this life! The hate was so deep they wanted to kill him!

Genesis 37:18-20 NKJV
18 Now when they saw him afar off, even before he came near them, they conspired against him to kill him.

19 Then they said to one another, "Look, this dreamer is coming!

20 Come therefore, let us now kill him and cast him into some pit; and we shall say, 'Some wild beast has devoured him.' We shall see what will become of his dreams!"

They then devise a plan to sell him instead of killing him, by selling him into slavery.

Genesis 37:27-28 NKJV
27 Come and let us sell him to the Ishmaelites, and let not our hand be upon him, for he is our brother and our flesh." And his brothers listened.

28 Then Midianite traders passed by; so the brothers pulled Joseph up and lifted him out of the pit, and sold him to the Ishmaelites for twenty shekels of silver. And they took Joseph to Egypt.

But Joseph knew he was special, because he had purpose and he knew deep down that he was going to do great things. I want you to know that you will go through some trials and tribulations in your life because of the anointing that is upon your life, but God's divine purpose is being manifested for his Kingdom purposes. Joseph eventually went to prison because someone lied on him, but God was still with him. I want you to that despite all that you go through, the Lord is with you!

While Joseph was in prison for three years, he prophesied to a butler that he was going to be released from prison, who then told Pharaoh about Joseph. Joseph then prophesied to Pharaoh that a time of famine was coming and God gave him prophetic wisdom in how to avoid the famine.

He told him how to store up 7 years of grain and assets so that the people would not starve when the famine came. As a result the Lord gave him favor with Pharaoh. Pharaoh ruled all of Egypt and put him in charge over all the affairs of Egypt. Joseph was second in command to Pharaoh!

Do you see the divine purpose of God in this story? Although there was much pain, God turned it around for their good and his glory! This is why Paul said, all things work together for good to them that love God! God used Joseph's pain for his divine purpose! This is how the Hebrew nation of Israelites came into Egypt, and he used Joseph as an instrument of his righteousness.

So through all the trials and tribulation, temptations and pain he went through, God blessed him abundantly. He went from the pit, to the prison, and to the palace. But guess what? It wasn't just for him.

Remember Joseph's brothers hated him, had him sold into slavery, and he ended up in Egypt, so when there was a great famine, all the peoples of that land including his brothers had to come to Egypt to get food. When they saw him they didn't know who he was. He eventually revealed himself to them, and as a result they realized their brother was alive and that it was all for a greater purpose!

Gen 45:1 Then Joseph could not restrain himself before all those who stood by him, and he cried out, "Make everyone go out from me!" So no one stood with him while Joseph made himself known to his brothers.
Gen 45:2 and he wept aloud, and the Egyptians and the house of Pharaoh heard it.
Gen 45:3 Then Joseph said to his brothers, "I am Joseph; does my father still live?" But his brothers could not answer him, for they were dismayed in his presence.
Gen 45:4 And Joseph said to his brothers, "Please come near to me." So they came near. Then he said: "I am Joseph your brother, whom you sold into Egypt.
Gen 45:5 But now, do not therefore be grieved or angry with yourselves because you sold me here; for God sent me before you to preserve life.
Gen 45:6 For these two years the famine has been in the land, and there are still five years in which there will be neither plowing nor harvesting.
Gen 45:7 And God sent me before you to preserve posterity for you in the earth, and to save your lives by a great deliverance.

Dear brother and sister did you hear that? God used Joseph's life as an instrument of his righteousness to fulfill a divine purpose. Listen to what he said in Genesis 50:23.

Genesis 50:19-21 NKJV

19 Joseph said to them, "Do not be afraid, for am I in the place of God?

20 But as for you, you meant evil against me; but God meant it for good, in order to bring it about as it is this day, to save many people alive.

21 Now therefore, do not be afraid; I will provide for you and your little ones." And he comforted them and spoke kindly to them.

Did you hear what Joseph said? His brothers meant it for evil, but God meant it for good. Why? To save many people alive! Now there is some great revelation in this story for you and me, Joseph is a type of Christ, or someone whose life was similar to that of Jesus Christ.

Jesus was the favorite of his father. Hated by his brothers the Jews, who lied on him, sold him for 30 pieces of silver, they had him killed by the Romans, and he was crucified, put in a pit which was the grave.

Theologians say that Christ went down into hell and preached to the spirits in prison held captive by Satan. He released the prisoners of the Old Covenant, rose from the dead after 3 days, came back to earth for a short time, then went back to the palace in the sky which was heaven!

Do you see the typology or symbolism that exists between Joseph and Jesus? Joseph suffered to bring about the divine purpose of God. Jesus suffered to bring about the divine purpose and plan of God as well through his death at the cross! Peter confirms it in the scripture!

1Pe 3:18 For Christ also suffered once for sins, the just for the unjust, that He might bring us to God, being put to death in the flesh but made alive by the Spirit,
1Pe 3:19 by whom also He went and preached to the spirits in prison,
1Pe 3:20 who formerly were disobedient, when once the divine longsuffering waited in the days of Noah, while the ark was being prepared, in which a few, that is, eight souls, were saved through water.

Jesus died for you and me. He paid the price for our sin, so that we would not have to die. Joseph saved his brothers, his family, and the nation of Israel and Jesus saved you and me. Joseph's brothers did not know who he was and he finally revealed himself to them.

One day, the Jews who many do not accept as Messiah, or recognize him as LORD and Savior will see him face to face and cry out to him, and will receive him, and accept him as LORD OF LORD'S, KING OF KINGS, and the CHRIST, who is THE SON of the LIVING GOD!

The story of Joseph and our LORD Jesus Christ are some of the most profound examples of divine purpose being manifested in the Bible. And just as God manifested it in the lives of them and others, he will manifest in our lives as well! Each and every one of us has a purpose and God will bring it to past in the assigned time that he has ordained.

One thing I have learned as a Pastor after many years in ministry is that the things God has predestined, purposed, planned, promised and prophesied belong to God. But there are things that we must do such as having a strong prayer life, being passionate about the things of God, understanding the balance of priorities in our life as it relates to family, work and home, pursuing purpose, and desiring to do the will of our God. We must also understand that the pain you have been through or presently going through is not just for you, but for others you may encourage, comfort, or minister too. Last but not least Jesus said that the godly in Christ will be persecuted in 2 Tim 3:10-12. Why? Because of the name of Jesus Christ!

I want you to know it doesn't matter who you are or where you are. God knows you by name and just as the Global Positioning System (GPS) gets you to your destination in a physical sense, God will use his divine purpose system to get you to the predestined purpose that he planned for you before the foundations of the earth.

Child of God I want you to know that God's Divine purpose system is at work in your life as we speak. Every step you have taken, everything you have been through, God is using it to divinely get you to a place in him where you will fulfill divine purpose in Christ.

Just like many Saints in the Bible, God is ordering your steps according to his Word, and he will use it for your good and his glory. So our prayer should always be LORD, not my will but your will be done in my life, and may your Kingdom come, and your will be done in earth, as it is in heaven, in Jesus Name! Amen.

About the Author

Pastor Jamal E. Quinn is the Senior Pastor of Firm Foundation Christian Fellowship in Riverview, FL. He is a native of Louisville, Kentucky and a decorated U.S. Navy veteran of 21 years.

He accepted the call into the ministry and was licensed as a Minister of the Gospel of Jesus Christ in 1999. After retiring from the military in Sep 2005, he returned home to Riverview, a community of Tampa, FL., where the Lord led him to start a community Bible study by faith, preaching, teaching and sharing the Gospel in his neighborhood to family, friends and anyone that had an ear to hear.

In Oct 2007, after faithfully serving in ministry for many years and conducting a Bible study group in his home, the LORD called Pastor Jamal and Prophetess Sheryl Quinn to plant Firm Foundation Christian Fellowship of Jesus Christ in the community of Riverview, Florida with a few faithful Bible study members.

Pastor Quinn is a shepherd, visionary, mentor, and watchman who preaches the Word of God with zeal, passion, power and truth. Pastor Quinn's passion is teaching, exhorting and encouraging men, women and youth to fulfill their God ordained destiny, and to live their lives as examples in Jesus

Pastor Quinn also worked in the commercial sector for nine years in Information Technology before being called to ministry. He is the author of five self-published books entitled: *"Seven Hindrances to the Blessings of God." "How Good and How Pleasant it is: The Importance and Power of Unity." "Speaking the Word of God by Faith." "The Power of Prayer, Prophecy and Praise" and "R" Daily Devotional: 40 Days of Restoration."* For additional information on these books, visit the website at https://jamalquinn.com/

He received his Associate of Science Degree in Liberal Arts at Excelsior College, Albany, New York, and his Bachelor of Arts in Pastoral Ministry from South Florida Bible College and Theological Seminary, Deerfield Beach, FL.

Pastor Quinn has been married to Co-Pastor and 1st Lady Sheryl Quinn, his high school sweetheart for over 35 years. For additional information on Pastor Quinn or Firm Foundation Christian Fellowship, visit https://www.firmfoundationcf.org

www.ingramcontent.com/pod-product-compliance
Lightning Source LLC
Chambersburg PA
CBHW071540040426
42452CB00008B/1070